To dear ⌖ W9-CJM-629

from The Sister

of St. Lucy Filippini

about whom This book

is written.

June 5 1979

Sister Margaret Peird,
m.P.F.

Forever Yes

Forever Yes

The story of Lucy Filippini

by

Sister Giacinta Basile, M.P.F.
and
Sister Geraldine Calabrese, M.P.F.

DORRANCE & COMPANY   •   *Philadelphia and Ardmore, Pa.*

NIHIL OBSTAT ....
Censor Librorum

Date ..June 6, 1978........

IMPRIMATUR ....
Bishop of Paterson

Date ..June 6, 1978........

Contents

Foreword

In his later works, Rembrandt took to portraying Christ in a fascinating way. He apparently sought to convey an idea of what Christ was like not so much from the expression he painted on the visage of Christ as from the expression he put upon the faces of the figures surrounding Christ in the picture. Consequently on those Rembrandt canvases one can come to understand the majesty of Christ and his compassion (as the artist conceived these) by reading the faces of the people who stand around him. It is they who declare the truth of Christ.

One might say that this has been the role of the saints in Christian history, to be like the figures in those Rembrandt paintings of Christ. While in this world they stand close to Christ, and their lives make a meaningful statement about him. They provide penetrating insights into the person of Christ and his mission. The careful reader will have the same sense of Saint Lucy Filippini. Her life and work disclose the power, the goodness and the joyous beauty of Christ. Lucy makes Christ more understandable to us.

—Reverend James C. Turro
Professor of Sacred Scripture
Immaculate Conception Seminary
Darlington, New Jersey

Preface

This book is more than a mere biography of St. Lucy Filippini. It is a reflection of a life in which all of us can recognize ourselves. In its pages are portraits of deep human experiences with nuances
—of faith, trust, abandonment;
—of loneliness, discouragement, weakness;
—of sensitivity, commitment, covenant;
—of depth, joy, peace;
—of anguish, controversy, persecution;
—of strength, docility, daring.
But it was Lucy's love for God and man that softened some experiences, highlighted others and ultimately blended all into a beautiful portrait—a portrait of a complete Christian woman.

This biography was shaped after many hours, days and months of study and prayer, of probing and prayer, of conversation and prayer. We looked at Lucy's life, her decisions, her works, her words through the eye of a contemplative camera—piercing time, culture and personalities.

We discovered a woman who transcends all time, a woman who speaks to women of all cultures, a woman who challenges all personalities to respect their dignity and beauty, to recognize their sacredness and power.

We believe that Lucy Filippini lived the title of this book *Forever Yes*. Contemplative by nature, Lucy was ever in tune with the Word of God within her, within others, and within every circumstance of life.

Her dynamic, prophetic, magnetic teaching, her openness to the moment, her gospel-rooted life—All evidenced her *Forever Yes*.

Lucy was an extraordinary woman . . . judicious, happy, practical, far-sighted, perspicacious! Her oneness in God gifted her with

wisdom   to clarify doubt,
courage   to proclaim justice,
zeal   to develop talents,
strength   to overcome all obstacles, joyfully,
freedom   to spend herself totally,
daring   to raise the dignity of women.

Yes, she was truly a prodigious woman!

Yesterday Lucy enlightened the dark corners of her world, as she penetrated the superficialities, the ignorance, the materialism of her age.

Today Lucy enlightens the dark corners of our world, as her teachers penetrate the superficialities, the ignorance, the materialism of our age.

Today, Lucy invites every reader to proclaim his own *Forever Yes*.

—Sister Geraldine Calabrese, M.P.F.

Acknowledgments

We are indebted to our fellow religious, our friends and students whose need and request elicited our work and whose questions helped to shape this biography.

We are particularly indebted to our Major Superiors, Sister Zaira Mastrini, M.P.F., and Sister Mary Paglia, M.P.F., for their thoughtfulness, their sensitive response and their enthusiastic support; to Sister Diamante Biagini, M.P.F., whose passionate devotion to Lucy introduced us to the real Lucy and stimulated us to grasp the essence of her being; to Sister Helen Ippoliti, M.P.F., for her keen editing of the first chapters, for her valuable suggestions, and for her warm response to each reading; to Sister Victoria Baccelloni, M.P.F., who opened new horizons to us as she gave us a personal tour of the first school sites; to our dear fellow-sisters in Italy—at Villa Maria Regina in Rome, in Bolsena, and in Procena for their warm hospitality during our eight-week stay in Italy in the summer of 1977; to Sister Patricia Martin, M.P.F., who typed the manuscript with devotion, patience, and care; to Sister Lucille Fitzpatrick, M.P.F., who served as copyist; to Sister Mary Dolores Ferrecchia, M.P.F., who edited the manuscript; to Sister Mary De Bacco, M.P.F., and Sister Lillian Picco, M.P.F., who proofread the manuscript; and to Mr. Nicholas Amatelli for the cover design.

Historical Overview

Lucy Filippini, a native of Tarquinia, Italy, was a prophet . . . a contradiction to her age . . . a woman ahead of her times. Her life spanned two centuries, the last half of the seventeenth and the first third of the eighteenth. Lucy Filippini lived in an era aptly labeled "baroque."

Baroque! It was an age which corrupted, vulgarized and popularized Renaissance naturalism. It was an era which applied Renaissance naturalism to sentiment and action without the restraint of Renaissance classicism.

Baroque! It was an age of excess, of extravagantly elaborate and grandiose ceremonies, of superficial religious sentimentality, of long and colorful processions, of superstitious rituals. In the world of fashions, styles were, to say the least, bizarre. Both in action and in sentiment, baroque culture scaled the vulgar pinnacle of ornate expression. It was an age of extremes!

It was the Counter-Reformation period. While secular artists mirrored and promoted the hedonistic culture of the day, Christian artists defended and affirmed their faith.

While Jesuistic humanists preached "all for the honor and glory of God," shallow-brained followers picked up the cry and corrupted its devout intent. Opportunists used the maxim to justify their actions. They reduced the lofty ideal to an artificial manifestation of excessive freedom and restraint. The Spanish Inquisition is only one example.

While Spain, France and Austria extended the confines of their empires, a great part of Italy lost its political independence. Only those areas under papal rule, the papal states, approximately one-fifth of the peninsula, retained their "national" identity and independence. During this time, the Church was also a temporal power in Italy. Ecclesiastics, delegated by the Pope, exercised both spiritual and temporal authority in the papal states. In the exercise of their roles as statesmen, churchmen often followed the same pattern of political coercion and opportunism set by the "national states" under the rule of Spain, Austria, France or other powers of the day.

Very often, young men became priests, not to spread the gospel but rather to fulfill their political ambition or to satisfy their desire for riches. The clergy, excessive in number, were the largest owners of landed property in every "Italian" state. As a consequence they enjoyed exorbitant privileges in judicial matters. Yet at the same time they held absolute sway over peoples' consciences. There was a superfluity of priests without a ministry, holding several occupations and employed in all sorts of profane tasks.

But as in every state of life, saints and sinners lived side by side. There were among the clergy sybaritic prelates and genuine ascetics, great men of letters and ignorant priests, dissolute or slothful monks and excellent teachers and zealous evangelists. Even in the monasteries a general slackness of discipline prevailed.

It was this epoch which gave birth to Cardinal Marc Antonio Barbarigo and Lucy Filippini. It was also the era that saw the growth in Italy of congregations preaching the most austere penances. Saint Paul of the Cross and Saint Leonard of Port Maurice, both contemporaries of Lucy Filippini and Cardinal Marc Antonio Barbarigo, literally obsessed by the memory of Christ's Passion, practiced the most rigorous asceticism. They were among the saints of their age—prophets—contradictions to their times.

Eight different popes ruled during this span of time. Among the eight, Clement XI, who held office from 1700–1721, stands out as the most progressive and most influential. He advocated the building of seminaries and the founding of schools for boys and girls. He also encouraged religious orders of women to continue educating girls within the confines of their monasteries. Every one of the eight popes, however, struggled to improve the moral and educational standards of his age.

In the early part of the sixteenth century Angela Merici, foundress of the Ursulines, organized a school for girls in Brescia, Italy. By 1641 the Visitation Nuns had already opened private academies for girls. Most often, however, these educational institutions were situated in or very near large cities and towns, and rarely, if ever, were they tuition-free. Consequently, the very poor in the cities and towns, the farmers and common laborers in hamlets and villages, found it either inconvenient or financially impossible to send their children, especially their daughters, to school.

When Pope Innocent XI assigned Cardinal Marc Antonio Barbarigo to the Montefiascone-Tarquinia Diocese in 1687, the Cardinal accepted the challenge gratefully. He knew the history of that papal state, was aware of its current misery, of its educational and moral decadence. Cardinal Barbarigo also realized that for thirty years this poverty-stricken diocese had been deprived of leadership; a Vicar had ruled the papal state from afar. The latter's sporadic visits had been perfunctory and ineffective. By default, then, the destiny of this forgotten papal state had rested in the strong grip of the powerful rich.

Class distinctions were extreme during these times. The very poor were a people abandoned, illiterate, immoral, hedonistic. An uneducated, apathetic clergy, further demoralized the people. Everywhere, among the very poor as well as among the rich, the Cardinal discovered unbelievable misery and corruption. But Cardinal Barbarigo was a man of strong faith and boundless trust in God's providence. So, fearlessly and courageously, he accepted the call to serve the very least of his brothers.

For the people of the Montefiascone-Tarquinia Diocese, October of 1687 marked a turning point in their spiritual and cultural life. To these abandoned people, an intensely dedicated priest had been sent, a man intimately acquainted with suffering and trials, a prophet who accepted challenges as opportunities to prove his all-absorbing love for God.

For the Religious Teachers Filippini of yesterday, today and tomorrow, however, the memorable point in time was, is, and ever will be January of 1688. In that month of that year, Cardinal Marc Antonio Barbarigo and Lucy Filippini met for the first time. In those moments in time, a new family was conceived, a community of Religious Teachers, dedicated to the Christian education of women and to the restoration of the family of Christ.

1

The Awakening of Corneto-Tarquinia

Love Divine come down to me!
Fill my heart with Thy sweet
flame, From my soul never
part!
—Lucy Filippini

JANUARY 21, 1688 dawned brisk and clear in Corneto-Tarquinia, Italy. A festive mood prevailed in the papal state. Today, Marc Antonio Barbarigo, recently assigned Cardinal-Bishop of the combined Montefiascone-Tarquinia Diocese, would visit his people for the first time.

Corneto-Tarquinia buzzed with excitement. Tradesmen closed their shops; farmers abandoned their work; townsmen decked their palaces and huts with flowers. Dressed in their Sunday best, children and young girls, carrying baskets filled with perfumed blossoms, lined the road from the gate to the Cathedral. Young and old, rich and poor—all awaited the arrival of their Cardinal-Bishop, their spiritual and civic leader.

Cardinal Marc Antonio Barbarigo's reputation had preceded him. The hungry, bedraggled Cornetans hoped for relief. They had heard of his boundless concern for the poor. He would be their savior.

The impoverished mothers breathed hope to their newborn babes. This man would feed them and clothe them. Stories of his benevolence towards indigent mothers and their infants were widespread.

The nobility was divided in its reactions. The God-fearing anticipated a much-needed reform. They had heard of his zeal in

1

eradicating ignorance and vice in Padua, of his courage in the face of insolence, of his refusal to compromise ecclesiastical authority in Corfu. This man of God would, they prayed, lift Corneto-Tarquinia from its dungeon of ignorance, sin and iniquity.

The immoral, degenerate nobles, on the other hand, were indifferent to his coming. Yet their curiosity compelled them to interrupt their particular celebrations to become spectators in the common one.

Apprehension, however, gripped the uneducated clergy; uneasiness clutched the hearts of the apathetic. Their apparent participation camouflaged their disquietude. On the other hand the long-suffering, virtuous clergy yearned for his coming. For too long, they had been lonely voices in the desert of this sin-filled world.

Lucy Filippini, surrounded by a group of animated teenagers, awaited him happily. Lucy had inspired her friends with admiration for the man by retelling anecdotes she had heard from her uncle—anecdotes of Barbarigo's nightly excursions to aid the abandoned, of his love for orphans, of his courage in the face of criticism.

Her words gave flesh to his image. Her desire to see him and to hear his voice increased with the telling of each story. Wrapped in her thoughts, she became silent. In her mind's eye, she relived the imagined dialogues she had had with him ever since she had heard of his impending visit. She longed for the actual encounter.

So all awaited his arrival. Today all Cornetans—the religious and irreligious, the rich and the poor, the lazy and the ambitious, the ignorant and the educated, the young and the old—all were one in their welcome, yet diverse in their expectations.

Church bells pealed their "benvenuto!" Marc Antonio Barbarigo and his small retinue of men, simply dressed, were approaching the town gate. The Cardinal, in contradiction to the spirit of the times, had discarded all pomp. He traveled with as few priests as possible, not wanting to inconvenience the parishes in Montefiascone nor to burden those in Corneto-Tarquinia.

In an epoch where baroque lifestyles flourished, the simplicity of the Cardinal was disturbing to the superficial, who numbered many in Corneto-Tarquinia.

As Cardinal Barbarigo made his way to the "duomo," he prayed for his people. He knew the work laid out for him in this old Etruscan town, dotted with churches and towers. He was well aware of the rampant immorality among the young and the old, of the numerous illegitimate babies left behind by the seasonal farmers who came to Tarquinia during the planting and harvest times. He knew that malaria orphaned even more. But the knowledge that saddened him most deeply was the clergy's ignorance of Christian Doctrine and their immoral lives, the scandals, the apathy. Their reform had to take precedence.

His mule ambled too slowly; he ached to begin. He would try every means to build up the Body of Christ.

He reached the square in front of the Cathedral, hailed and cheered in true Latin manner. He looked upon his people lovingly, intensely. A hush fell. Cardinal Marc Antonio Barbarigo's powerful voice filled the square. Briefly he explained the purpose of his pastoral visit. He had come to serve, not to be served. He was their father; their problems and their joys would be his. He had come to give succor to the poor, to provide homes for the homeless, to instruct all in the truths of the faith. Together they would restore the kingdom of God in Corneto-Tarquinia.

His stay would begin with a five-week mission to be preached by the Lazarist Fathers. He urged his listeners to attend. He would be available to them, to listen to their problems, to help them in whatever way possible. His sincerity rang loud and clear. Many recognized it and felt hope.

Although all heard his message, each responded according to his own disposed will.

The first few days of the mission reflected the general impiety of the Cornetans. Very few attended the services; fewer went to confession. Cardinal Barbarigo attended every function, prayed constantly, fasted rigorously. Only God could convert these people, and convert them He would. The Cardinal never lost faith.

Gradually the number increased. Word spread that the preachers were interesting; more people came. The number gradually swelled to two thousand. Slowly God's word began to take root. Many were reconciled; public sinners begged forgiveness of their neighbors. The confessional boxes were never empty. The Cardinal continued to pray ceaselessly, to fast rigorously. He praised God for his bountiful mercy.

On the last day practically the whole town attended the solemn Pontifical Mass celebrated by the Cardinal. With his own hand the Cardinal distributed Holy Communion to the two thousand people who had made the mission. That same afternoon he closed the mission with the solemn procession of the Most Blessed Sacrament through the streets of Corneto-Tarquinia.

His zeal gave him energy. The seed had been sown; it needed only to be nourished. He would begin by establishing a school of Christian Doctrine with the clergy from Montefiascone as instructors. Tomorrow, however, he would begin his interviews. Most of his people would clamor for material aid, and some would seek spiritual comfort. A few would ask for guidance in their life-calling.

Lucy Filippini would be among the latter. The pastor had already pointed out Lucy to the Cardinal and had confided that she taught catechism for him. With obvious pleasure, he had insisted that Lucy taught the class better than he ever could. The Cardinal smiled at the note of pride in the pastor's voice. This young woman, the Cardinal thought, deserved close observation. Lucy, the pastor continued, had been orphaned at an early age. Together with her brother, Francis, and sister, Elizabeth, she lived with the maternal aunt's family. They were from the noble Picchi-Falzacappa family.

Cardinal Barbarigo had been praying for Lucy as he waited for her to come in. Lucy walked gracefully into the room. Her eyes, enormous in her face, were bright but intense. The Cardinal immediately sensed her inner turmoil and her need to talk.

They appraised each other and sensed a common bond. An immediate rapport was established. Lucy knew she had found a father and friend. Without hesitation, therefore, she poured out

4

her soul. For some time now, she confessed, she had known her life's vocation—to dedicate herself to God alone—as a religious, perhaps.

But, Lucy continued, her sister Elizabeth, whom she loved dearly, concerned her. Elizabeth, Lucy noted quietly, was a lively, young woman very much influenced by the customs and fashions of the day. Her aunt and uncle found it difficult to discipline Elizabeth. Not that her sister was bad, Lucy hastened to add. It was merely that Elizabeth loved good times and beautiful clothes. More than anything, Lucy feared Elizabeth's daily association with her superficial friends. If Elizabeth would only agree to board with the Benedictine Sisters at the Monastery of St. Lucy, then Lucy would be at peace. Daily contact with the good nuns would bring out the best in Elizabeth. Elizabeth, Lucy sighed, had tremendous potential for good.

Lucy's words and tone of voice bespoke gentility, compassion and deep sensitivity.

Elizabeth, she continued, was more than a sister to her. She loved her as tenderly as a mother loves her only child. Separation from her would be heartrending. This she would suffer, however, if she could be assured of her sister's well-being. Her eyes pleaded help. Her young soul radiated the intensity of her love for God and for her sister.

The Cardinal was impressed by her warmth and candor. He was moved to compassion by her obvious struggle. This girl-woman loved deeply; she would suffer much. She was so different from other girls her age; she was single-minded, God-centered. The Cardinal had met a kindred soul. He sensed their lives would be closely interwoven, saw her as indispensable in his reform movement. How this would take place, he did not know, but that it would, he had no doubt.

With each passing day, Cardinal Barbarigo became more and more convinced that God had great designs for Lucy. He felt responsible for her, so he decided to keep her close to him. He would be her spiritual director; he would help her to discover God's will for her.

5

In her frequent encounters with the Cardinal, Elizabeth also learned to trust him. He was a good listener; he encouraged Elizabeth to unburden herself to him. When the Cardinal finally broached the idea of her boarding at the Monastery, Elizabeth accepted the suggestion and promised to consider it. Convinced he wanted only what was best for her, Elizabeth finally agreed to do as the Cardinal asked.

Lucy and her relatives found words inadequate to express their gratitude to the Cardinal.

So, with the consent of the aunt and uncle, the Cardinal accompanied Elizabeth to the Monastery of St. Lucy in Corneto. There she would also enjoy the companionship of her cousin, Anna Picchi. Furthermore, the Cardinal promised the concerned relatives that he would arrange a good marriage for Elizabeth, which in effect he did.

Lucy was peaceful now. Her beloved sister was happy and well taken care of.

Therefore, when Cardinal Barbarigo returned to Montefiascone that July, Lucy went with him. Her spiritual father would place her, at his own expense, in the monastery of St. Clare. This holy place was to be her home for the next four years.

2

The Unfolding of New Life at the Monastery

*He who seeks solitude escapes
three dangers . . . those of
sight, hearing and evil speaking.*
—Lucy Filippini

THE CARRIAGE RIDE across the marshlands from Tarquinia to Montefiascone must have seemed endless to Lucy Filippini. The separation from Elizabeth and from her relatives had been painful. Her heart ached with love and longing for her sister. Only the thought that Elizabeth was safe with the good Benedictine Sisters in the Monastery of St. Lucy eased the pain of her loss. Lucy recalled with nostalgia the many beautiful hours she had spent in the monastery. It was in that monastery that she had made her first Holy Communion. There she had learned to read, write and do needlework. But, more importantly, it was there that Lucy had grown to understand, from the example of those Sisters, the power of womanhood fully developed.

Now she was traveling to another monastery in another town, the Monastery of St. Clare in Montefiascone. She would be alone among strangers, her first time away from home and family. Only the reason for her going there softened the pain somewhat and calmed her fears.

Lucy's thoughts turned next to the Cardinal, her protector. She had chosen to come to Montefiascone at the suggestion of Cardinal Barbarigo. For the first time she had found a person who inspired her full confidence. Only he, Lucy felt, could provide the spiritual

7

guidance she needed at this time in her life. She desired nothing but to dedicate herself totally to God. But how? In what state of life? Where? How could she best prepare herself to know and follow God's will for her? She knew the answer: she had to deepen her spiritual life, perfect her needlework and other feminine skills, and use her talents in the service of others. Joyfully she would live out her waiting period. She had nothing to fear. Her God-sent counselor would be near to guide her; she trusted him implicitly. Her thoughts rested lovingly on her good friend. Peace and serenity filled her! How grateful she was for him.

In the meantime, the Cardinal was reviewing his own thoughts and feelings concerning Lucy. Looking beyond Lucy's youth he envisioned the woman-grown, the missionary, the reformer. No doubt she would require occasional pruning. But, he mused, what Lucy needed more of was continuous nourishing. Her brilliant mind had to be challenged; her leadership qualities had to be developed. She was God's gift to his diocese, of that he was convinced. Montefiascone needed women like Lucy. He prayed for Lucy, whom he believed God had entrusted to his care. He prayed for guidance, for insight, for prudence. Someday, Lucy would work side by side with him—someday—in God's good time.

The end of their journey interrupted their individual reveries. There before them loomed Montefiascone, sitting like a queen on her mountain throne. The steep ascent to the town matched Lucy's excitement; soon she would cross the threshold of her new home. One thing followed quickly upon the other. Someone knocked. An old sister opened the huge door, and Lucy found herself inside the monastery. Everything fell into place. She experienced a deep peace; she was home.

The whole community had gathered to welcome the Cardinal and Lucy, his protegé. Lucy greeted each one warmly. The three oldest sisters looked upon her hopefully; perhaps this young woman would bring them the sunshine they so sorely needed.

Sr. Chiara Felice Mereanzi, the Superior, asked one of the younger sisters to show Lucy to the boarders' dormitory on the third floor. On her way Lucy noted with pleasure the individual choir stalls lining the corridor leading to the dormitory. Her heart burst with gratitude; she would have her private trysting place with her beloved Jesus!

Upon entering the large dormitory, which Lucy would share with several other boarders, she ran to the window to contemplate the magnificent panorama below. It was breathtaking! How could she find words to describe this enchanting beauty to the people back home! Her window overlooked the crystal-blue Lake Bolsena with its two islands—Martana and Bisentine. The peaceful and sunny towns of Marta, Capodimonte, Valentano, Gradoli, Grotte di Castro and San Lorenzo, famous for their ruins of castles and palaces, loomed like sentinels scattered about the vast region. The crater lake, the largest in Italy, stood flanked by a succession of woods, vineyards and lonely beaches. Lucy broke into song, praising God for His beautiful world.

Pulling herself away from the splendor below, Lucy began to settle her belongings, fix her bed, arrange her night table. She had decided to leave her best clothes and fineries in her valise. She would use only the simplest dresses and no ornaments at all. She had noticed the comparative poverty of the other boarders. She did not want to flaunt her wealth, nor did she want to embarrass the young women.

When the domestic responsibilities were assigned by the Superior of the Monastery, Lucy accepted her charges gracefully. No task would be too menial nor too difficult. She had come to learn and to serve; she would employ no measuring stick. She found it difficult to contain her joy as she began her new life in search of her future.

It was easy to love Lucy. Her face alight with happiness, she went about her work singing softly, anticipating needs, unobtrusively completing chores left undone. She was a shaft of sunlight in that dark monastery.

Soon, however, Lucy became painfully aware of the irregular observance of the established schedule. Very few attended the liturgical hours. Some of those who attended did not participate. Later, when the nuns knew Lucy better, they admitted to her their lack of education; several could neither read nor write. Poor

9

unhappy women, thought Lucy, locked into a life not of their own choosing, or having chosen it, suffering disillusionment or discouragement. She pitied their emptiness. She prayed for them and loved them. Her openness to them encouraged a few to approach her and ask her to teach them to read and write. Lucy, with the sensitivity of a gentle woman, made the service seem a favor bestowed on her.

Skillfully, Lucy made the reading lessons become experiences in the art of meditation. The youthful teacher would ask her students to explain the message contained in the reading. Her simplicity made it easy for them to express their thoughts. They felt free to question her; they were drawn to her like a magnet. Her gestures fascinated them; her words pierced their hearts; her exuberance lifted them.

No wonder, then, that Lucy became their confidante. To her they lamented their abstemious meals, the prolonged hours of prayer, the too-exacting schedule. Lucy listened and felt compassion.

But while some complained about the austerity of the life, her elderly nun-friends bewailed the lack of austerity, the loss of fervor. They (Sr. Lucy Frangiotti, Sr. Faustina Rose Clementini, Sr. Catherine Celese Tacchini) clung to and longed for the return of the original spirit. How many times Lucy sat at the feet of old Sr. Lucy and listened to her tell and retell the origins of the monastery. Her old voice trembling with emotion, Sr. Lucy recalled how five public sinners, moved by the zeal of the saintly Capuchin, Father Modesto, had resolved to lead penitential lives. For the benefit of any nun who might be listening, her old voice would quiver loudly, relating how the first group had lived a life of real poverty and outstanding severity. The town had been edified! The noble women had sent their daughters there to be educated. Many had remained. The community had grown. However, when the spirit of poverty no longer prevailed, the downfall of the community had begun. They needed a reformer, they insisted, someone who would lovingly but firmly lead them back to the former spirit. Lucy heard the plea and felt compassion.

When the Cardinal came to visit her that week, Lucy shared with him the anguish of the old nuns, as well as the pain of the others. What could he do to alleviate the one and the other? The Cardinal, marveling at the growing maturity of his spiritual daughter, filed away the insight for the time being. He would consider it that night, in the privacy of his room.

The Cardinal was proud that Lucy could look beyond the problems the nuns were experiencing and yet continue to appreciate all she was learning from them. Eyes sparkling, Lucy admitted that her needlework was improving; that she had begun to capture the art of cooking; that she could now be sensitive to the fatigue induced by cleaning house. For all these blessings she was grateful.

But over and above all these accomplishments, Lucy continued, she valued the hours set aside for prayer and meditation. The Lord was teaching her so much about herself. Humbly she confessed her imperfections, especially her vanity. She was still so attached to her beautiful clothes. True, she had refrained from wearing the very stylish dresses in her wardrobe. But, she admitted shyly, she did keep them near her bed, and she did enjoy looking at them often.

The Cardinal listened lovingly; he recognized the inner struggle. He admired her self-pruning, but he did not elaborate on the subject. Lucy would come to grips with her avowed vanity. He praised her, instead, for the generosity with which she used her talents with the nuns and encouraged her to do even more. He invited her to extend her service to those outside the monastery as well—to teach catechism for him, to visit the sick and the bereaved, to reach out to the young girls who needed counselling.

Lucy's eyes sparkled her willingness. Of course she would! To spread God's love, to serve his people, these were her only ambitions!

Lucy's vigorous response encouraged the Cardinal to describe his own pastoral activities among his clergy and people. The seminary he had founded was thriving. The number of worthy applicants was growing. The periodic conventions he held for the continued education and spiritual renewal of his clergy were beginning to show results. Parishes were coming to life. Though his schools for

11

Christian Doctrine needed more teachers, they were progressing beautifully. Yet, there was so much more to be done. He begged Lucy's prayers, gave her his blessing, and left.

That night, the Cardinal pondered the state of affairs at the monastery. What should he do? Should he mitigate the rule? It was worth a try, he thought. And so it was that in November of 1688 the Cardinal presented the nuns with a more lenient rule which reduced the long hours of prayer, improved the menus (allowing meat more often), and increased the hours of rest. Hopefully a degree of fervor would be restored. The monastery bells rang out the joy in the hearts of everyone.

Lucy lived each day eagerly, accepting whatever challenge the day presented. Every day during her free time she went out to visit the sick and the bereaved whose names she received from the good Cardinal. Another boarder always accompanied her. Lucy prepared hot broth for the sick, washed them tenderly, cleaned their rooms. Her words pierced their hearts; her compassion healed their hurts. The bereaved were consoled, their bitterness washed away by her depth of understanding.

Each day introduced Lucy to new tragedies, to indescribable poverty, to deplorable ignorance. The streets and alleys of Montefiascone became the finishing school where Lucy learned how to live charity and chastity radically. Chastity for Lucy became charity in action; it meant love and tenderness, compassion and heroic sacrifice. Chastity embraced all of God's children.

Lucy felt compassion for the poor women who knew so pitifully little about their faith, who appreciated hardly at all their worth as co-creators of the human race, who understood not at all the importance of their role in society. She grieved for the immorality among the young girls for whom life held only one fascination— flirtatious sensuality. Lucy suffered to see the very young growing up like weeds, with no one to teach them. There were still too many children, she thought painfully, who did not attend the school of Christian Doctrine. Now she understood better the Cardinal's distress. He had accomplished so little in the face of so much that needed to be done.

Lucy drew the young girls to her by teaching them needlework. Then, very sweetly, she would introduce their favorite subject— love. Love, she would say, was the greatest gift one could give another. And in marriage the gift reached its perfection and became a sacrament, a witnessing to the union which exists between Christ and His church. A new life opened before these young women. Lucy captured not only their hearts but also their wills. Every day they gathered around her, listening, asking questions. Love took on greater depth of meaning for them. Many sought her out for private counselling at the monastery.

The sight of ragged girls her own age accomplished what no sermon could have achieved. Her finery, her beautiful and expensive dresses pleased her no longer; in fact, her wardrobe actually embarrassed her. How could she possibly permit herself so much luxury in the face of such dire poverty? But her sensitivity to the self-respect and pride of the young girls restrained her from disposing of her riches as mere alms to beggars. Instead she made use of feastdays, birthdays and special holidays as opportune occasions to give away her possessions as gifts to beloved friends.

"Signora Lucia," as the townsmen called her affectionately, became a familiar figure to both the rich and the poor of Montefiascone. All who knew her loved her and sought her advice.

Happily, Cardinal Barbarigo followed Lucy's growth. Lucy had found herself, he thought. God's designs for her were taking shape. Lucy was approaching twenty; soon she would have to decide the road she would follow in life. Gently, but firmly, the Cardinal very often hinted at this to Lucy.

Lucy entertained no doubt whatsoever concerning her vocation; she belonged to God totally and forever. Her apostolic spirit, however, continued to resist the monastic life; yet her contemplative nature rejected a life outside the monastery. She needed a "monastery without walls."

3

Confronting Her Fears

*I seek the glory of God and in
doing this, I fear no obstacles,
no matter how great.*
—Lucy Filippini

THE YEAR WAS 1691 . . . the season, autumn. It was the fourth year of Cardinal Marc Antonio Barbarigo's episcopacy in the Montefiascone-Tarquinia Diocese and the third year of Lucy Filippini's residence in the Monastery of St. Clare. It was the first year of Innocent the XII's pontificate.

New life was coursing through the veins of the diocese served by the Cardinal. The tiny papal state was definitely on the upward move toward Christ—becoming—growing. But Cardinal Barbarigo, the man responsible for the dynamic reform movements there, was not satisfied.

It was a climactic autumn evening in 1691. The Cardinal was returning home from the seminary, where the boys and young men of his diocese were receiving a sound Christian education, where a new generation of men was being formed.

Every visit to the seminary convinced him more forcefully that womanhood had to be sanctified simultaneously. He had already made several attempts to establish schools for the girls, but each endeavor had failed. The teachers he had called in from Rome and elsewhere had lacked the perception needed. But the Cardinal's determination to actualize this resolve had never wavered.

The home, the very root of the social ills in seventeenth century society, had to be penetrated. The mother, the very fountainhead

14

of the home, had to be reformed. The schools he was determined to establish would prepare tomorrow's mothers. From early childhood, girls would be taught the truths of the Christian faith, the science of the saints and the art of domestic living. As fully formed Christian women, they would become the reconstructive elements of society.

As he walked, his thoughts quickened his consciousness of everyone and everything around him. On this particular evening in the autumn of 1691, the Cardinal's sharpened senses not only saw and heard, but pierced the sights and sounds of his surroundings. What he perceived and detected strengthened his resolution.

The town was awakening from its siesta. The various odors and noises announced themselves distinctly to the passersby: shops reopening, children shrilling their games while munching large slices of bread, women chatting and clicking their knitting needles, church bells chiming the *Ave Maria,* scattered groups of old people praying the rosary. The Cardinal blessed his people lovingly as he passed among them. He prayed a prayer of gratitude for the yearly missions, for the schools of Christian Doctrine, for the Seminary, all of which were touching the lives of many of his beloved people.

He recognized, however, the dire need to effect more, to go deeper, to touch the very roots of humanity. His heightened perceptivity sensed the struggle for supremacy present in those other sounds, those other sights: immoral love songs, raucous laughter, coarse language, vulgar gossip, high-pitched quarreling voices, illicit lovemaking, indecent dress, neglected youngsters, frivolous mothers. The Cardinal's face revealed his soul's agony. His eyes burned fiercely, caught between tears of frustration and tears of determination. He had to establish free schools for girls; he had to find the right teachers. Humbly he willed a strong prayer to God the Father. Tired lines etched his face; contemplative suffering hallowed his eyes. He was lost in God.

Gradually the Cardinal became aware that he was no longer walking alone. Focusing his attention, he recognized two Jesuit Fathers alongside him. They were traveling to Rome, he heard them say, and had decided to stop in Montefiascone to visit the

15

famed Seminary. Apologizing for his seeming discourtesy, the Cardinal greeted them cordially and offered them hospitality.

During the evening meal, the Cardinal felt impelled to share his proposed school project with his guests. The mutual response was electric! The Cardinal's face lit up as the Jesuits poured out the success story of a certain Rose Venerini of Viterbo. Under the direction of Father Martinelli, a member of their society, Rose had already established Schools such as the Cardinal had described.

God had heard the Cardinal's plea. This was the appointed hour.

Wasting no time, the Cardinal wrote two letters: one to Father Mayroni, temporarily replacing Father Martinelli, and the other to Rose Venerini.

For some time now, Rose had entertained the thought of establishing Schools elsewhere. Therefore, the Cardinal's invitation to found a School in Montefiascone served as a confirmation of God's will.

Letters of acceptance reached the Cardinal, both from Rose and from her director, expressing joy that was edged, however, with certain reservations. Rose's stay in Montefiascone, of necessity, could not be permanent; her first responsibility rested in Viterbo, with her nascent Schools. She would remain in Montefiascone only until she found and trained someone to replace her.

The Cardinal agreed with the stipulations made, confident that Divine Providence would intervene. Solicitously, the Cardinal provided comfortable transportation for Rose and her companion at his expense. Since the Cardinal preferred that Rose feel free to rent and furnish a Home-School, according to her own taste and experienced needs, he made temporary arrangements for lodging in the Monastery of Saint Clare.

Lucy Filippini and Rose Venerini would live under the same roof for a time. Was this premeditated? Did the wise Cardinal have an ulterior motive? Had he already singled out Lucy to succeed Rose? Who really knows? But whether the move was spontaneous or planned matters little, really. What makes it noteworthy is that it was providential.

Lucy was drawn to Rose from the start. Here was a woman who had the courage to pioneer a new way of life for women. Rose, a sedate sixteen years Lucy's senior, read the questions piling up against each other in Lucy's mind. Rose appreciated the interest of this vibrant young woman. She wondered about her.

One evening Rose, taking Lucy aside, explained how the School had evolved. She had wanted to be a religious, she said. Her confessor, however, had advised her to remain in Viterbo to work for the good of her neighbor. She had begun by inviting women and young girls to join her in praying the rosary. It was soon evident that some of them knew neither the prayers nor the mysteries. So the prayer session had become a catechism class. Later, with the addition of the domestic arts, the School had gained in popularity.

Rose admitted that it had not been easy at first; free Schools for girls were unprecedented. It was natural, therefore, that she had had to bear derision and calumny. But God had given her the strength to face criticism and had provided human support in the person of her spiritual director, Father Martinelli. Finally, the School needed no justification; her students provided proof enough.

Several months elapsed before Rose and her companion found a house for rent, furnished it, propagated the idea of a School, and took registration. During this time Rose and Lucy shared many precious moments together. The acquaintance ripened into a friendship which would be life-long. Rose was deeply impressed with young Lucy. Her spiritual depth mystified her; her instinctive teaching talent interested her. She had noted Lucy's patience with the nuns and admired her respect for the individuality of her nun-students. She recognized Lucy's mature acceptance of herself as a woman and understood why Lucy's advice was sought even by laywomen. Her beloved friend, Rose thought, was a very special person, a spiritual prodigy. She would make a great Teacher!

Early in the year 1692 Montefiascone was about to witness another first—the opening of a free School for girls. To insure the best possible education, Rose Venerini had limited the number of girls in the class to forty. The curriculum included the study of Christian Doctrine, reading, writing, church music and the domestic sciences.

The changes effected by the School were, to say the least, dramatic. In fact, the Venerini students were easily identified by townsmen and foreigner alike by their behavior and modesty, by their frequent reception of the Sacraments, and by their zeal for the Christian faith.

Every day, and sometimes twice a day, the jubilant Cardinal came to the School to praise and to encourage the teachers and the students. For the good Cardinal, this was the hour of the Transfiguration and "it was good to be there!"

However, while the School in Montefiascone was flourishing, the School in Viterbo was crumbling. Father Martinelli, in whose hands Rose had entrusted the Schools, had been transferred, depriving the Viterban Schools of leadership. Rose was in a quandary: Either she had to return or Father Martinelli would have to be restored to Viterbo. It was Cardinal Barbarigo's gratitude which provided the solution to her problem. When the Cardinal asked Rose how he could repay her for the good she was doing in Montefiascone, Rose needed no time to formulate her favor. Would he use his influence, she begged, to have Father Martinelli reassigned to Viterbo? Her Schools would collapse if one of them were not there. Her deep concern, plus the Cardinal's own fear of losing her, prompted immediate action. The Cardinal, who was highly respected, succeeded in affecting the transfer. Father Martinelli's influence did restore peace in Viterbo, but only temporarily. An underlying concern continued to predominate in the occasional letters he wrote to Rose.

Rose became progressively convinced that, in the very near future, she would have to return to Viterbo. Her replacement for the Montefiascone School would have to be found soon. This person would have to be instructed, supervised and encouraged in the use of the method. Her replacement would have to be not only a Teacher but also the Directress of this School and of all the future diocesan Schools the Cardinal planned to open.

Rose's prayer for guidance in this matter always brought before her mind one person—the same one each time—Lucy Filippini. Lucy was intellectually gifted, talented in the domestic sciences, deeply spiritual, and, Rose thought tenderly, a woman despite her youth. Lucy, however, would have to come to grips with her own paradox: her strongly contemplative but equally apostolic nature.

Rose knew her choice was good and knew, somehow, the Cardinal would agree. So, with resolute step, she headed towards the Monastery. It was only fair that she speak to Lucy first.

Lucy greeted Rose affectionately; it was always a pleasure to see her friend. Rose, a woman of few words, came to the point quickly. Would Lucy assume the responsibility of directing the Schools of Montefiascone? Rose would remain for a time to instruct her, to help her to solidify the founding Schools. When the time came, she would accompany her to the other towns also. Moreover, she would maintain close contact and would be available any time she needed her.

Lucy's ponderous "no" suffocated her spontaneous "yes," but Rose chose to hear the first response, the "yes." She courteously but firmly dismissed each objection raised by Lucy: incapable . . . too young . . . inexperienced . . .

Rose handled each tormenting question calmly. Lucy was well-educated, talented. Youth had advantages: It attracts the young; it has abundant energy. Lucy had been teaching since she was twelve, had continued to teach in the monastery. So Rose refused to hear the "no"; she continued to hear only Lucy's instinctive reply, her unguarded *"yes."*

Rose felt obliged, therefore, to submit Lucy's name as her only choice. Rose Venerini's discerning recommendation restored harmony to the Cardinal's troubled soul. He had no doubt, of course, about Lucy's capability. Therefore, thinking only of the well-being of his School, he resolved to call Lucy from the monastery and to appoint her Directress of his present and future diocesan Schools.

Four years had passed since that eventful day when Lucy, trusting her Cardinal, had left home with one preponderant purpose—to discover God's Will for her. How deep were God's designs would soon be revealed by the very man she had chosen for her spiritual director. And the Cardinal, confident that he was reading the signs of the moment correctly, called Lucy "to go forth and teach."

Lucy was crushed under the weight of the call. She previsioned anguish and trials converging upon her from all sides, making it impossible for her to distinguish one pain from the other.

"What shall I do?" she cried. "I shall ruin everything. I shall destroy a valuable work." How could she dare undertake such a responsibility? How could she follow Rose's sure step? All the light in her soul extinguished; she was blind with fright, insecurity, doubts. What future did this new way of life promise? Where would it all end?

Barbarigo patiently heard her cries, assured her steadily. He would never abandon her—neither in life nor in death. She had spent her youth, he reminded her, preparing for this challenge. Would she now turn her back to God's call?

Lucy's heart bled to see the beloved Cardinal's concern for her and for his Schools, conscious that only her consent could dispel his anxieties. From the depth of her darkness, experiencing no consolation—either from her own convictions or from her God— *Lucy quivered her "yes."*

Her farewells at the monastery scraped open every fear. She would never again enjoy the security of these walls. She would never again experience the peace of an ordered life, of a prayer-filled day, of long hours of intimate communication with her God; she would no longer delight in the company of her religious family. Emptiness drained her as she separated herself from these cherished women.

Flushed with excitement, the Cardinal awaited Lucy's arrival at the school. Now he would move quickly to what he considered a very important matter: the designing of a habit for Lucy and her Teachers.

Insensitive to Lucy's femininity and fine taste, the Cardinal roughly designed a habit which Monsignor Jerome Berti cut out, using very coarse material. Neither realized the distaste Lucy experienced when she handled the crudely designed habit she was given to sew. Despite her repugnance for the tasteless style and the coarse material from which it was made, Lucy donned it, grasping only too well the profound meaning of this investiture.

Externally, Lucy appeared calm, serene; internally, a tempest raged. Each school day dragged on, endlessly tedious, insupportable. Her agony grew as she wrestled with fierce temptations "to live like other women . . . to abandon this way of life . . . to flee from the danger of dissipation school brings."

In the midst of the storm within her, Lucy prayed quietly, joylessly, desperately seeking the God who seemed so far, far away. In spite of the darkness within her, Lucy's fidelity to prayer never wavered. Her faith in the hidden God gave her the strength to present herself serenely to the world. Her constant hope in God's loving wisdom fortified her to hide her internal ravages, especially from those whom she had committed herself to serve.

Gradually, however, the conflict between Lucy's frail body and her tortured soul erupted, and the body succumbed. At first the sickness seemed passing, but shortly it appeared mortal. She lost her appetite; her body swelled; a slow, constant fever developed. But until she could hide her malady no longer, Lucy continued to teach.

Lucy's health as well as her internal struggle troubled the good Cardinal. The Cardinal loved Lucy like a daughter and was convinced that only she could administer his schools successfully. He spared no means to help her. With no regard for expenses, he sought the best doctors, directed holy men her way to console and uplift her.

Lucy's sickness, which persisted for more than a year, provided the time she needed to sort things out, to discover and remove the obstacles obstructing the light. Painfully, Lucy began to scrutinize her reactions—the underlying causes for her behavior. She groped her way to the bottom of her being with question after question.

Why did she fear the responsibility imposed upon her? . . . Slowly, but with cutting honesty, she searched. Did she fear criticism? Was she afraid of failure? But then, on whom did she really depend? On herself alone? or on God? Her probing furrowed a clean cut; a tiny ray of light trickled through.

Painfully, Lucy confessed her pride, her lack of dependence on God, her lack of trust in His divine providence.

Day after day Lucy faced her weaknesses. Humbly she admitted her faults. Nothing was impossible to God. In Him and with Him even she, Lucy, could do all things. Healing tears trickled slowly down her face, purifying her inner hurts, removing her insecurities.

Courageously, Lucy probed deeper. Other questions had to be asked. Honest answers had to be made.

Why did she reject the School apostolate? She blushed with shame at this question. Had she not been a teacher, and a successful one at that, from early youth? Yes, she had been successful; she had to admit the truth.

Determinedly, she continued the examination. Did she need the security of the monastery to be dedicated to God? Why was she afraid that her apostolate would be total work? What did prayer really mean to her? What was prayer? Could not prayer and work be so related as to become one?

This probing carved a deeper cut . . . an excruciating wound . . . admitting an even brighter light. Copious tears, healing waters of hope, washed away larger hurts, greater fears. Meekly, Lucy confessed her fear of a life without the security of an established order, her myopic vision of prayer, her superficial understanding of apostolic love.

With each self-revelation, a degree of peace and serenity returned. Her spirit nourished her body; her health began to improve. Though physically weak, Lucy emerged spiritually strong from the self-confrontation, unafraid of the future, sure of her vocation in the School apostolate. Even as a convalescent, she returned to her classes; her love for her students compensated for the physical strength she lacked.

Both the Cardinal and Rose Venerini had been patient, kind, and supportive throughout the long-suffering experience. Lucy's gratitude to each would take an eternity to express.

Lucy soared in the weightlessness of her new found freedom. In the brilliance of her restored vision, God's designs for her were now radiantly clear. Exultantly, Lucy boldly proclaimed her *fiat:* Wherever He led her, she would follow trustingly. No longer did she fear to assume the leadership of the schools, never again would her *fiat* be a quivered whisper . . . never again!

4

Founding Her First Schools

*What great work the Lord has
entrusted to us women.*
—Lucy Filippini

A REGENERATED Lucy Filippini—freer, bolder, stronger—
emerged from the long purgative combat. With decision and
courage, this apostle set about to actuate as much as divine inspiration and the illuminative voice of the Cardinal suggested to
her. Vigorously and confidently, Lucy now assumed her role as
leader.

One common vision united Cardinal Barbarigo and Lucy
Filippini: the restoration of Christian family life. The School would
achieve this goal as it educated the woman from childhood to old
age. Therefore, Lucy's School would be a classroom, not only for
children, but also for women—single, married, widowed, young
and old, rich and poor. In fact, the School in Montefiascone (and
this would be true of all the Schools) had one room set aside for this
very purpose. In this room, Lucy held prayer workshops which
took place in the very early morning and again in the evening to
make it possible for poor farm women to attend. In Montefiascone
an adjoining room and the stairway to the Schoolhouse ac-
commodated the overflow of women who attended.

The workshops began with vocal prayer, followed by a lesson on
Christian living. Lucy's presentation was always so clear and
simple that even the dullest among them learned. A step-by-step
meditation on the gospels came next. Lucy concluded the sessions
with the exhortation that they be witnesses to what they had prayed

and that they put the light of their faith to work. Her words transformed; even the hardest among them softened. Her example prompted them to become involved in new and magnificent battles within the home as well as in the social apostolate. Through these adult education classes, Lucy became one of the first women to dedicate herself to the reformation of her times.

The religious subjects most often developed by Lucy were the Nativity of the Lord God, the Passion and Death of Jesus Christ, the Sacramental Jesus, and the Mother of God. Lucy's love and devotion for her Lord and Savior and for her Beloved Mother excited the hearts of her listeners and inspired them to emulate her in her devotions.

The mystery of Bethlehem was one of Lucy's favorite devotions because of its one simple message, *Love*. During one Christmas Novena Lucy gave the women of Montefiascone the following meditation:

A child is born to us. What do I see? The monarch of heaven hidden in a humble dwelling; the first-born of the Most High wrapped in stiff straw! . . . Why does the supreme King of Glory have a cave for a palace, a manger for a throne, poor clothes for his purple and two animals for his court? . . . Will he who feeds a world of creatures depend upon the breast of a virgin?

A child is born to us. While He is the great, in fact the greatest, He has made Himself small for us; though rich, He has made Himself poor for us.

. . . He lies on the hay that we might tread upon the stars. He whimpers among animals that we might converse with angels. He trembles in his nakedness to clothe us with light and immortal glory . . . Oh, divine, most ingenious love! You changed the immutable God from a lion to a lamb, from a thunderbolt to a flower, from a Lord of vengeance to a Prince of Peace, from monarch of angels to a servant of men.

Yet, who would believe it? That love which overcame the omnipotence of a God does not have the energy to overcome the ingratitude of men. . . . Most divine Infant, with a ray of your loving glance shatter the hardness of our hearts . . . Give us strength never more to offend you and a heart always ready to love you.*

*Pietro Bergamaschi, *Vita della Venerabile Lucia Filippini*, vol. II. (Italy: Bagnora-Scuola Tipografia, 1916), pp. 47–49.

Central to the workshops for women, however, was the School for the young. Lucy understood deeply what her work among the children meant, what her delicate mission was. She looked beyond the child and beheld a young woman, a wife, a mother, a teacher, or a religious. This precious being placed in her care carried within her the promise of the next generation—a great potential for good or for evil. In this conceived vision lay the singular significance of the School. The knowledge of God and His truths, the formation of conscience, the woman's noble but grave responsibility as co-creator of the human race, the woman's unique role as builder of society—these were the sacred lessons that God entrusted to Lucy and her Teachers to impart. Lucy realized vividly the importance of the home where the child received her first formation. However, the School, Lucy would tell her Teachers, must reinforce the good, eradicate the errors, fill the void, and build for the future.

Lucy's gentle leadership created in the School a home-like atmosphere of a profound Christian family where all was regulated by faith . . . where the presence of God dominated . . . where Christian principles permeated the whole day.

Rose Venerini basked in the success of her friend. She no longer feared returning to Viterbo. True, she had initiated the School as envisioned by Cardinal Barbarigo. However, it was Lucy who was establishing it, solidifying it, and giving it a character all its own. The Jesuit-inspired method used by Rose Venerini in Viterbo was the same one utilized in Montefiascone except for a few minor modifications introduced by the Cardinal. But a method is intrinsically tied to the personality of the teacher who employs it. Into the form given her, Lucy breathed her own fervor, her student-centered concern, and her docility. The method reflected Lucy's simplicity, her sense of dignity and her refinement, and above all, her *sense of mission*.

Lucy, keeping in mind the child's short attention span, arranged the time schedule accordingly. Work (sewing, spinning, or knitting) alternated with prayer; the lesson (reading, writing, or basic arithmetic) with meditation, the rosary, or another devotion;

silence with the singing of spiritual hymns. Lucy taught Christian Doctrine three times a week, using the question and answer method from the Bellarmine Catechism, and simple questions and answers on the practical aspects of Christian living. Religion was taught as a way of life, however. It filled the whole day; it was not relegated to a specific time.

Lucy loved her children into becoming all they could be. Her task, however, was not easy. Her students came from homes culturally, economically, and spiritually deprived. It required inexhaustible patience to stretch the horizons and enlarge the minds of the uncultured. It demanded boundless endurance to reach the dull-witted. To hold the attention of her students, Lucy made her classes interesting by encouraging student participation, by using visual aids to reinforce the spoken word, and by using the lab method more frequently than the lecture method.

But it is the manner rather than the method, she would tell her Teachers-in-training, that makes all the difference. Her example spoke her convictions. With a gentle and gracious manner she performed her teaching duties diligently and lovingly.

Eagerly, the Cardinal looked forward to opening Schools throughout his diocese. Lucy shared his zeal. In discussing this possibility, however, they agreed that the Teachers would have to be not only well-trained, but what was more important, well-grounded in their Religious-Teacher vocation. They had to be aflame with apostolic zeal.

Lucy, whose responsibility it had become to prepare Teachers, did everything in her power to impress her neophytes with the sublimity of their mission. She possessed that rare gift that knows how to communicate spirit. Her own deep sense of mission inspired the same in her followers.

To allow her Student-Teachers the opportunity to experience, beforehand, the life they proposed to embrace, Lucy provided them time for observing and practice-teaching while she guided, supervised, and corrected them. Firmly but gently she instructed them:

The Teacher should patiently bear with the little immodesties and foolishness of children and the crude mannerisms of the unlearned . . . In handling teenagers and adults, the Teacher should prudently and tactfully spare them confusion and embarrassment . . . The Teacher should pray constantly for her students! . . . The Teacher should be lively and enthusiastic, but at the same time serious and modest, as becomes the dignity of the subject she is teaching.

Lucy knew intuitively when a girl did not have a true vocation. With the delicacy of a noblewoman, she directed her elsewhere without causing her embarassment.

Within a short or longer period of time, depending on the individual's readiness, several young women were eventually invested as Religious-Teachers. Among them was a certain Vincenza, a mature, deeply spiritual woman. Both the Cardinal and Lucy singled her out as an excellent candidate for the new School in Corneto-Tarquinia. The Cardinal suggested that Vincenza and Lucy "team teach," with Lucy taking the leadership responsibility.

Lucy's happiness exploded; her own townsmen would now be beneficiaries of the School. She knew, only too well, the pressing exigencies of her native town. She would be going home to serve her own people. Elizabeth, now a happily married woman, would be there. What joy to be near her again!

The Cardinal went ahead to Tarquinia, where he met with Nicolo Cesarj, the Vicar General, to make the necessary preparations. Understanding the urgent needs of Corneto, the Cardinal had decided to found a boarding school for the poor girls, a day school for the other poor, and an orphanage. He would place the direction of the three foundations on Lucy, and the spiritual direction of the boarding school on his vicar general.

The Cardinal, with great concern for the comfort of his Teachers, finally found accommodations which he furnished simply but completely. Delicately, he thought of those small things so important to women. The house, situated in the school building, boasted a library—complete with books on pedagogy and spiritual reading. The Cardinal, however, never felt he had done enough for his Religious-Teachers.

When everything was in order and ready, Lucy and Vincenza—accompanied by the ever-vigilant Rose Venerini—arrived in Corneto-Tarquinia. Lucy's homecoming was a jubilant occasion for the townsmen; Rose marveled at Lucy's efficiency and self-confidence. Lucy needed her no longer, she thought proudly. Soon she could return to Viterbo. (When the Cardinal later opened Schools in the Bolsena area, he and Lucy cordially continued to invite Rose to join them. She always accepted the invitation graciously, eager and ready to support her young friend.)

The classroom arrangement in Corneto, like the one in Montefiascone, reflected the philosophy of its founder. The School was a sanctuary where children came to learn how to live as Christians. To know, love and serve God and His people took precedence here. Therefore, each classroom contained an altar, artistically covered with a silk or linen cloth, upon which rested a large crucifix. Fresh flowers adorned the altar. The image of Mary, to whom the School was dedicated, graced every classroom. To impress upon the students the sacredness of the School, orderliness and silence were required.

Here, as in Montefiascone, the School enrolled the entire female population. Here also, Lucy's interest in her students did not begin and end in the classroom during the designated school hours. Her concern followed them on the street, in the fields, within the home.

Constantly she reminded them that a great dignity was theirs; they were children of God, ransomed by His Son—made man; that they were members of God's family and they must therefore show respect for one another; that they must walk, talk, act with dignity everywhere—on the street, in their homes, in the church; that they were apostles—their singing of popular spiritual songs was part of their apostolate. Their parents worked hard; they owed them honor and obedience.

When Lucy visited her students' homes, she inquired about their behavior. The parents, appreciating the concerned interest, held back nothing. If the misdemeanors were the normal pranks of children, Lucy counseled patience; if the matter were of a more serious nature, she took immediate action. She corrected firmly, instructed kindly, inspired repentance.

Whenever her students committed a wrong, they dared not meet her searching glance; they recognized her intuitive powers. Lucy, however, did not avoid them; she approached them, talked to them lovingly, inspired their confidence, taught them to forgive themselves and others and to accept forgiveness.

Teenagers found her a wonderful listener. Filled with scruples, they ran to her—anxious, afraid. Her wisdom, softened by empathy, calmed them, enlightened them, helped them mature. Lucy's healthy regard for her own sexuality freed her and enabled her to understand them, to explore with them the meaning of love and how to treasure it and preserve it. Adolescence was a difficult and delicate stage, and delicately Lucy guided the young ladies into womanhood.

It was in Corneto that Lucy opened her School to still another phase of life—that transitional time from the single state to the married. It was here that she initiated the Spiritual Exercises for brides-to-be. For eight days Lucy housed the future bride, educating her on the duties and responsibilities of the married life, leading her in prayer and meditation, giving her practical hints on everyday living. Lucy's concern, however, did not end with the eight-day retreat. She remained close to the bride, following her growth into wifehood and motherhood.

The Cardinal beamed his happiness; the "School-Without-Walls" was effecting a good without parallel. Corneto-Tarquinia's future was being molded there. Humbly the Cardinal thanked God for Lucy and her Teachers. Without them, he would be a man without arms and feet; in them, he was multiplied, many times.

Encouraged by the obvious success of the School, the Cardinal and Lucy concentrated on the orphanage. Their hearts ached for the poor neglected children orphaned by death or by uncontrolled passion. If it had not been for Lucy's uncle and aunt, whose home had become hers at the death of her parents, she too would have suffered the pains of the abandoned. Her prayers blessed her beloved relatives. Providing for these homeless ones would be her constant act of gratitude to God for her love-filled childhood.

The orphanage in Tarquinia harbored nineteen children that first

30

year. Lucy lost her heart to them—forever. Even when her numerous responsibilities weighed heavily upon her, Lucy remembered them. When she no longer lived among them, she remained present to them with her constant concern and continued benefactions. Every time she visited Corneto, the orphanage was her first and last stop. But never did she go empty-handed; her motherly instinct told her what to bring: candy, toys, pretty clothes, holy articles. Lucy's solicitude for the orphans continued even after they left the shelter of the orphanage.

The story of Catherine Valentini is but one incident among many. Lucy heard of the girl's plight. Catherine wanted to marry but had no dowry. Lucy's generosity reached out to protect Catherine's honor. In those days it was a dishonor to marry without a dowry. She bequeathed her own dowry to her in the following words:*

November 14, 1718—Montefiascone

I, the undersigned, in finding myself at an advanced age still firmly resolved not to become a nun, nor to marry, but (with God's grace) to continue to live as a Religious-Teacher until death, renounce and assign all my dowry, which had been set aside for me, to the honest young woman—Catherine Valentini—poor orphan, raised in our school.

. . . Signed by my own hand,

In faith—Lucy Filippini

Lucy's charity, as well as the Cardinal's benevolence toward the orphans, encouraged the townsmen to follow their example. The vineyard which the Cardinal had purchased in Tarquinia was large enough to feed the community of Teachers, students and orphans, and to have a surplus to sell at harvest-time as well. The people of Corneto donated grain and wine; twice a week they offered bread and money. Nicolo Cesarj was edified by his townspeople.

In her beloved Tarquinia, Lucy Filippini's days and nights ran into each other. Lucy, together with her companion, had set solid

---

*Pietro Bergamaschi, *Vita della Venerable Lucia Filippini,* vol. I (Italy: Bagnora-Scuola Tipografia, 1916), p. 164.

foundations. Vincenza could now continue the good work begun, along with another Teacher Lucy would assign. Lucy had to return to Montefiascone to continue her duties as Directress, to prepare other Teachers for other towns.

So, after bidding farewell to her dear orphans, her students and to Elizabeth, whose help had been invaluable, Lucy traveled once again across the marshlands—back to Montefiascone.

5

Forming Contemplatives-in-Action

> *My daughters, give alms and*
> *refuse no one, because it is*
> *charity which sustains our*
> *schools.*
> —Lucy Filippini

STRUCK BY LUCY'S energetic response to the times, earnest young women felt impelled to follow her. Some of them had attended the retreats she gave in the various towns of the diocese; others had heard about her and her work from Cardinal Barbarigo or from their pastors. All had come together, to the novitiate, for one reason; they had been captivated by her heroic spirit and wanted to emulate her.

Lucy's whole life can best be described as a dramatic love affair with God. The intensity of her prayer-life, as well as the magnanimity of her work-life, continuously expressed her ardor. His truths she cherished; her Jesus, God-made-man, she adored; Mary, his tender mother, she treasured.

During those joyless hours at the beginning of her apostolate, Lucy had turned to Mary, the Mother of Sorrows. At her feet, Lucy had found the courage to accept the cross of her own suffering. It was during those nocturnal days that Lucy had finally conceived the deeper meaning of obedience. Mary had taught her! Love for Mary, her heavenly Mother, filled Lucy's heart, overflowed and touched the souls of her aspirants. Mary became their Queen Mother also; the novitiate, her sanctuary. Every day they chanted the rosary and prayed the office of Our Lady in Italian rather than in Latin so that the candidates could absorb what they prayed. A commentary on the Psalms, contained in the office, deepened their understanding along with their appreciation.

In the novitiate, the celebration of Mary's feast days was a contemplative reality affirming Mary's predilection by God and her supremacy in their lives. Lucy's spontaneous praises and prayers mingled with the ingenuous expressions of love and devotion of her Student-Teachers.

Each year, on one of her feast days, Lucy and her little community made a pilgrimage to the sanctuary of Our Lady of the Oaks in Viterbo. They walked the sixteen kilometers from Montefiascone to Viterbo praying, singing, enjoying one another's company. Their noon-day respite in a clear wooded area restored them and reinvigorated their spirits. As they knelt before Our Lady's image in Viterbo, their fatigue vanished completely. They had so much to confide, so very much to ask of her. Especially did they entrust to her maternal care their benefactor and friend, Cardinal Marc Anthony Barbarigo.

During his frequent visits to the School and novitiate, the Cardinal begged them to place the needs of the church and of his diocese in Mary's hands. He encouraged them to persevere in their vocation. The church of Montefiascone awaited them!

With them he shared his concerns about his abandoned people, the neglected poor in the small towns and hamlets in the Lake Bolsena area. Monastery schools, the only educational institutions in Italy at that time, could not financially subsist in the small towns and hamlets; the poor could not afford to send their girls to school. Therefore, these unfortunate people were deprived not only of secular education but also of religious instruction.

It was their unique privilege as Religious Teachers, the Cardinal reminded them over and over again, to open Schools in those regions up to now deprived of all educational opportunities, both secular and religious. As Religious Teachers, they would impose no financial burden on their people. They were to support themselves. Their Schools would be tuition-free and open to women of all ages and social standing. Their sacred mission was to transform society through the Christian formation of women.

Particularly did the Cardinal anguish over Capodimonte and

Marta, two small towns dotting the shores of Lake Bolsena. His pastoral visits to these places had confirmed his resolute intention to open a School there immediately. He found it difficult to wait patiently; he had to urge Lucy to ready four Teachers immediately. Those poor God-forsaken towns needed help desperately. With determination, the Cardinal approached the small community home where Lucy lived with her Student-Teachers. He would place his plea before her once again.

Lucy and her community always welcomed the Cardinal warmly whenever he came to visit, but today Lucy sensed a different excitement in him. Without delay the Cardinal informed Lucy he had a favor to ask of them. The young Student-Religious gathered around him, interested, alert. His visits energized their apostolic fervor; they yearned to be sent. The Cardinal's eyes embraced them. They were his hope; they would transform his diocese, restore it to God. He shared his burden with them, introducing them to Capodimonte and Marta. The plight of those towns was not new to Lucy; she had already given retreats there. How well she understood their need! Lucy was in full accord with the Cardinal; her Religious-Teachers had to go, very soon! Yet, they could not go until they were ready!

In principle, the Cardinal agreed with Lucy; the Teachers should be very well prepared. But the needs of his suffering people prompted him to speak his concerns hopefully. He began by locating the towns on a map, hanging on the wall of the study room. Capodimonte, the Cardinal explained, was a victim of its own natural beauty and resources: its ideal location near the rich Bisentine Islands, its wooded area, its delightful climate and fresh air. This enchanting peninsula, mirrored in the lake, made a perfect vacation place for the Farnesi family. Here they came every year to hunt and carouse, bringing with them cavaliers, elegant women, comedians, musicians, august personages, and yes, sad to say, unscrupulous priests and prelates. The peninsula was reduced to a noisy playground of feasting and immorality. The residents of the town aggravated the situation; they stopped all work to join the merrymaking.

The Cardinal paused, reflectively. Only the School, which would

35

form the next generation, could effect a lasting change. His voice aroused their zeal. They longed to go now, immediately!

The retreats Lucy had given had touched many women; the School of Christian Doctrine had reached many more; but only the School could strike the roots of all of tomorrow's families.

The Cardinal gave Lucy an imploring look. When would her Religious-Teachers be ready? Did she have two, at least, to send? This was the favor he was pleading!

In the days and nights following, Lucy searched the minds and hearts of her disciples. Had they grasped the full scope of their mission? Had they learned how to merge prayer with work? Had they understood the unlimited horizons of their apostolate?

Lucy intensified her prayer—she needed guidance from above! Nine prayer-filled days later her eyes rested on two young women; they were the most mature among her candidates.

That spring of 1694 witnessed the move. Lucy, her two newly invested Religious-Teachers, and Rose Venerini traveled to Capodimonte. The School, a five-room house, opened its doors to the girls and women. The restoration of Capodimonte had begun.

Marta would be the scene for the next school-opening. Attentively, the mission-minded Teachers listened as Lucy painted a verbal picture of that little fishing village, three kilometers distant from Capodimonte. Lucy's eyes searched those of her students as she continued. Capodimonte was a picturesque town: its homes lapped on one side by the waves of the lake; its land covered with green chestnuts. Unfortunately, rampant immorality marred its beauty! Fishermen wasted their week's earnings on drink, neglecting their families and leading dissolute lives. Employers, whose only god was money, strangled the poor. Young men and women desecrated the church, making it the scene of lovers' rendezvous. Desecration reached its climax, however, on May 14th of each year—the feast of Our Lady of the Mountains. Pretending to honor Mary, the townspeople transformed the House of God into a house of traffic. A procession, characteristically baroque, formed in the church courtyard. Fishermen, tradesmen, farmers, professionals, carrying the product or symbol of their labor, tramped into the church, to the tune of their wives' strident acclamations: "Long live my husband's trade!" The statue of Our Lady at the rear of the parade punctuated the mockery. Correctly, the neighboring towns had nicknamed the extravaganza the *Feast of Barabbas.*

The Cardinal, Lucy continued, had used every tactic to put an end to this travesty but to no avail. Every attempt had been met with rebellion.

Lucy's account elicited varied responses. Some felt righteous anger! Others pained deeply! Still others pitied the people's ignorance! All, however, determined to make reparation for the offenses committed! Everyone hoped to be assigned to Marta.

Several of the aspirants were ready for investiture—ready to be sent. Yet which two for Marta? Who had the energy required for this mission? Who had the stamina, the courage? Lucy prayed deep into the night.

The next morning two happy women were called and invested. Eventually, they left for Marta, accompanied by Lucy and Rose Venerini. Marta, however, would not be dented easily. It would require measureless patience, constant self-renunciation and zealous prayer. Lucy would visit Marta very often; her abiding concern would bolster her teachers' courage in the difficult days ahead.

Within the next few years almost every town on Lake Bolsena would have a School, marking a turning point in the history of Italy.

The years 1694–1706 saw more than thirty young women seeking admission into Lucy's pioneer institute. Extraordinary women! They had to be! They were harbingers of a new state of life in the church. It was unheard of in that century that women live the religious life outside the cloister. Never before had women lived with and worked among the people as Religious-Teachers, as preachers in public places, as social workers. It was unheard of that good women should seek out sinners, wherever they happened to be. Following Lucy Filippini, the dauntless trailblazer, required vision and courage. These women, called to an exceptional apostolate, had to be endowed with the understanding of human nature, with mercy for human weakness. They had to be well-educated, deeply spiritual, Christ-centered women.

Being a practical woman, Lucy converted her novitiate into a laboratory where theory blended with action. Her aspirants practice-taught as well as observed, took turns to give the early morning or night meditations to the women, taught Christian Doctrine, and accompanied Lucy as she brought the school to the people. Here their curriculum was every facet of human experience.

Every day Lucy and a companion visited the poor who were sick, comforting them with food, love, and prayer. Every type of suffering aroused Lucy's sympathy. A woman whose daughter had committed adultery—grief stricken over the disgrace brought to the family—refused to eat or drink and turned her back on God. The story reached Lucy. Immediately she went to the woman to console her; to assure her of God's mercy, to induce her to eat. The woman turned a deaf ear. Lucy persisted day after day. As adamant as the woman was to continue in her despair, so was Lucy in her hope to heal her. Lucy's docility conquered! The woman forgave her daughter and herself; she was reconciled to God. Lucy's aspirants marked well her love-infused actions.

"My daughters," Lucy would say repeatedly, "give alms; don't deny anyone. It is charity which maintains the Schools." Lucy's life substantiated her directive. One day she noticed that several merchants were returning home, their wares unsold. Though Lucy had no personal need of their products, she proceeded to buy everything. Her two-fold charity gladdened the poor to whom she distributed the goods and relieved the no-longer dejected merchants. Turning to her companion, she reminded her that today they had fed and clothed the poor Christ. Lucy's gracious giving of alms took away the sting of receiving charity. Her kindly face and friendly words raised the spirits of the recipients and inspired them to give gratitude to the Giver of all Gifts.

"Judge not! Be merciful! Not once, nor twice, but always! Let God be our Model; consider His boundless mercy and forgiveness!" These were the basic Christian maxims Lucy stressed. Her own actions confirmed her words.

On one occasion Lucy met a woman from Siena who, to support herself, had turned to prostitution. In her, Lucy perceived the frightened little girl seeking security. Approaching her, Lucy touched the woman lovingly and invited her to go home with her. Moved to tears, the miserable woman accepted the invitation. She was too hungry and exhausted to question this concern for her. After a hearty meal, served by Lucy, the poor prostitute felt a gnawing need to unburden herself to this gentle woman whose eyes spoke only love, understanding and compassion. Quietly Lucy listened, wondering: Had this woman ever been loved purely, just for herself? Had she experienced the joy of God's personal love?

If there were only one extra room, Lucy thought, this lost soul could stay here with us. But there was no room in this house. Then Lucy thought of the Cardinal. He would find shelter for her. Lucy, however, wanted the privilege of instructing her and introducing her to Christ, Whose love heals all hurts. Together they went to the Cardinal. Without hesitation, he made arrangements for her to live in the Monastery of St. Clare at his expense. Lucy, however, would teach the dear woman Christian doctrine, sewing and the other domestic sciences. The woman would remain at the monastery until she was prepared to provide for herself.

Everyday Lucy taught her. The poor woman learned more than the lessons Lucy explained so well. She met the merciful Christ Whose blood had washed away all sin. She learned how to love and be loved. Her self-respect restored, the woman then returned to Siena. The bishop of that city was notified beforehand of her arrival by the Cardinal. Lucy never broke contact with her.

In 1698 Montefiascone suffered a very severe winter, causing great hardship. The very poor—women and children in particular—had insufficient clothes to weather the cold. Lucy did not rest until she could remedy the situation. Again she appealed to the Cardinal. His response was spontaneous and generous. He had all the heavy red drapes in his house removed. With the material, Lucy and her novices made clothes for the poor unfortunate. Again they had been privileged to clothe the naked Christ.

Cardinal Barbarigo admired Lucy's sensitive charity. As his

almoner, she had the freedom to extend aid to the needy without asking his permission. She had but to send him the bill at the end of the month. Each week the Cardinal placed an order with the baker for twenty to thirty pounds of bread to be given to any family who presented a note signed by Lucy.

Lucy's gentility towards and respect for old people was edifying. The old, she would say, were witnesses to the past, the representatives of family traditions, the foundations of the family. Lucy revered them. Across the street from the School in Montefiascone was a hospice which took in convalescents dismissed from the hospital. The home also welcomed pilgrims on their way to Rome. In Lucy's day a very old woman, Virginia of Valentano, was in charge. She was conscientious, but her advanced age impaired her efficiency. Lucy felt her pain. Very often, when the guests were many, Lucy and a companion helped her to clean, cook, and serve. Lucy stopped by every day to offer a consoling word and to check on whether or not she needed anything. Her companions would remember this lesson forever.

Lucy Filippini's lab-novitiate produced well-prepared Religious-Teachers; it graduated dynamic apostles.

Between 1695 and 1704—nine years—nine more schools were opened! It was a momentous time in the life of the church . . . and in the lives of two remarkable people—the co-founders.

Two by two the Religious-Teachers were sent into the small, neglected towns to minister to the very poor. Everywhere they became integral to the community with whom they lived, prayed, and worked. Everywhere they continued to serve the total female population, without the limitations of boundaries.

Valentano, Arlena, Tessennano, San Lorenzo, Gradoli, and Celleno were among the first of the Bolsena towns to receive the Religious-Teachers. Incredible was the transformation!

Latera was a charming town, 510 meters in altitude, surrounded by chestnuts and perfumed by laurel, rich with natural resources of mineral water and sulphur deposits. The Laterans, however, were characteristically lazy, unambitious, vindictive drunkards! Even the women drank too much. Here Lucy assigned Frances Brunotti whose tact and prudence, she hoped, would win over the quarrelsome and elevate the woman. Lucy's concern dissolved in the warm response the Laterans gave her Teachers. Latera was a consolation.

The people of Piansano were deeply religious and affectionate. Anna and Laura Lottieri, two saintly sisters assigned to the School, were loved and esteemed. Everyone praised their work; the pastor blessed them, gratefully.

Grotte di Castro was a picturesque little town, noted for its fruits and wines, for its staircases outside the houses and for its frequent earthquakes. Its people were gentle, loving, industrious and religious, noted for their fidelity to the Roman pontiffs. They were said to be articulate, open, democratic, and hospitable. The School in Grotte di Castro, staffed by Lucrezia Amari and Marcellina Marsile, bore abundant fruit.

Cardinal Barbarigo's interest and pride in the Schools never fluctuated. He wanted to be kept informed so that he could meet every emergency or simple need immediately. He visited the Schools often, checked the attendance, was concerned with the students' progress. He loved and was loved! The children crowded around him, kissed his hand, pulled at his garments. His face glowed pure joy; their innocence touched him deeply. His whole being rejoiced.

Clement XI, who had been elected to the Chair of Peter in 1700, considered Lucy Filippini's free Schools for the neglected female populace the most powerful forces for good in the Cardinal's reform movement. In fact, Pope Clement XI regretted the Cardinal's reluctance to found Schools outside his own diocese. Each request from the Holy Father called forth the same response from Cardinal Barbarigo:

"Someday soon, God-willing, but not yet. Let us deep-root them here first."

Lucy's constant solicitude, united to the Cardinal's, gave the Schools the stability and security they so much needed in their infancy. But Lucy, the visionary, prepared her Teachers for the day when their Schools would cross the borders of the diocese!

Lucy Filippini's religious family grew in number and in strength of purpose. In her wisdom, Lucy knew the source of that strength. Her community had a common vision—the Christian restoration of the family through the Christian education of the woman. She knew how important it was never to lose sight of that common goal. It was her responsibility to nurture the bond and keep it strong.

Twice a year, at least, she visited every School; more often, if there were the need. Twice a year, Lucy called her Religious-Teachers back to Montefiascone to be renewed in body and soul. Thus did Lucy sustain and preserve the original spirit.

6

Establishing a Unique Community

*I would spare no effort and I
would gladly give my life a
thousand times, that God might
be perfectly known and loved by
all."*
—Lucy Filippini

IN ONLY FIVE YEARS Cardinal Barbarigo's reform movements
had touched and changed the everyday life of his people. The
Seminary he had founded was already noted for its excellence; he
had organized on-going theology classes for his clergy, adult classes
for laymen and laywomen, Christian doctrine classes for everyone.
Every year he had made his pastoral visitations; he was acquainted
with every pastor and parish, knew their problems, helped them
solve their difficulties. Every city, town and village had benefited
from at least one five-week mission a year. But what pleased him
most were the schools and his Religious-Teachers.

From the height of these accomplishments, Cardinal Barbarigo
appraised the Schools. It was impossible to tabulate either the
immediate or the far-reaching spiritual, moral and civic good
achieved through them. He could never measure their worth; their
value defied human estimation. Firmly he resolved to do everything
in his power to ensure their future. Among other considerations, he
had to assure every School stability of residence.

The Teaching Community of Montefiascone, above all, deserved
this guaranteed status. Every year, since its inception in 1692, the
Teachers had had to transfer from one location to another; no
neighborhood wanted the School within earshot. The Cardinal

could not tolerate the situation any longer. A permanent Home-School had to be purchased, one large enough to serve as motherhouse, novitiate, center for the spiritual exercises and School. More and more women were seeking admission into the Teaching Community; more and more women were attending the spiritual exercises; more and more girls were frequenting the School.

Other factors compounded the need for stability even more. The Teachers scattered throughout the diocese deserved a home-base, a place to return to for the semi-annual retreat, for the vacation periods. The sick needed a place in which to recuperate; the old, somewhere to retire.

With his mind's eye, Barbarigo took a comprehensive view of Montefiascone, and each time the conclusion was the same; the ideal location was none other than the Monastery of St. Clare. This building, though old and in need of much repair, answered every requirement—and more. The monastery was connected to the adjacent parish church by an inner passageway, a practical feature which would facilitate the Teachers' spiritual ministry to the women and to the children. At the moment, the Teachers were situated a considerable distance from the parish church.

What would happen, however, to the nuns now living in that monastery? Sorrowfully, the Cardinal reviewed the efforts he had already exerted to help them. When Lucy was still a student there, he had mitigated their rule, hoping that a less structured, less-severe life-style would transform their sour dispositions, but to no avail. What action should he take now? Should he suppress the order? It would be no loss to the church of Montefiascone. Their way of life was not an inspiration to his people. His pastoral heart, however, considered the fate of the old nuns there. Where would they go? He couldn't put them out! He would have to wait and search, pray and trust in Divine Providence for the answer to his dilemma.

The superior of St. Clare's Monastery, Sister Chiara Felice Mereanzi, supplied the providential breakthrough. Through her confessor, Father Luca Antonio Miselli, Sr. Chiara begged permission of Cardinal Barbarigo to join Lucy Filippini. Sr. Chiara declared she could no longer bear the miserable living conditions at the monastery. Impulsively, Cardinal Barbarigo consented to the plea placed by Sr. Chiara through Father Miselli. But on reflection the Cardinal conceived what he considered a superior solution. Would it not be better to transfer Lucy Filippini and several of her Teachers to the monastery? With Lucy as the superior, the monastery could function both as the Motherhouse for the Teachers and as a second School for the townswomen and girls! The nuns could affiliate themselves with Lucy's congregation. As members, they could lend their services to the School according to their capabilities. In return, the Cardinal would make the needed repairs and would provide continued maintenance.

To make it easier for the nuns to consider the proposal freely, the Cardinal gave Father Miselli the task of presenting it to the nuns. Sensitive to the delicacy of his mission, Father Miselli explained the Cardinal's design and intentions prudently and hopefully. The material benefits attached to the plan drew an enthusiastic assent from the nuns; they yearned for relief from their miseries.

Characteristically, the Cardinal acted promptly. Together with his chaplain, Father Gabriel Gentili, and Father Alessandro Mieli, a member of the Fathers Operai (the Pious Fathers), he called upon the nuns at the Monastery of St. Clare. The community of nuns, gathered in the Chapter Room that 6th day of October 1704, were anxious to hear the Cardinal's proposal firsthand. They wanted to be sure of the promised benefits. Carefully they weighed the alternatives. They had nothing to lose, they thought. Their enthusiasm gladdened the unsuspicious and weary Cardinal. Only one nun dissented; Sister Mary Angel Piacentini. The Cardinal placed no obstacle before Sister Mary Angel, who preferred to affiliate herself with the order of Benedictines in Tarquinia. Graciously the Cardinal made arrangements for the transfer.

Certain of the nuns' consent and confident that the merger would prove beneficial to the nuns and Teachers alike, the Cardinal then proceeded to inform Lucy about his plan and the nuns' acceptance of it. Lucy agreed to the experiment, her eyes wide open to the precariousness of her position. Her nun-friends would find the transposition of roles hard to take: their one-time student now their Superior and Directress of Teachers! Yet she could not refuse the Cardinal. Steeped in God, thirty-two-year-old Lucy accepted this new yoke of service in faith.

Abandoning herself peacefully to the present, Lucy joined the Cardinal in his plans to solemnize the occasion. An eight-day spiritual retreat in preparation would be most appropriate. Lucy Filippini's Teaching Community interrupted its School Apostolate, and the Religious Community in the monastery suspended its regular schedule; both groups came together to unite themselves in prayer and hope-filled expectation. On October 15, they would become one community: the Religious Teachers of Cardinal Barbarigo. The prayerful waiting period came to a climax with the celebration of the liturgy by the Cardinal, the investiture of the nuns as Religious Teachers, and the conversion of the Monastery of St. Clare to motherhouse for the Religious Teachers.

The evening of October 15, 1704 saw the documentation of the activities of the day. With great solemnity, Cardinal Barbarigo presented the written rule to his Religious Teachers. Thus was established an innovative community with canonical status, an institute where women dedicated to God's service lived the evangelical counsels without vows. The women gathered in the Chapter Room, listening to the rules formulated by the Cardinal, were, of course, unaware of their history-making move; their lives were wrapped in their present "yes" to their beloved Lord and God.

Prayer and work, mortification and modesty were the key words to their lifestyle; Jesus Christ was their model for living the evangelical counsels. They were to teach Christian Doctrine, give meditations to the women morning and evening; operate Schools for girls (according to the method laid down by Cardinal Barbarigo); give spiritual exercises to women; and be active in parish ministry. They were to be evangelists!

Their specific role was the formation of new generations of women, educated and strong in their faith and keenly aware of their unique responsibility as women, upon whom the health of a God-centered civilization depended. Their constant goal was the restoration of the Christian family.

On the 27th day of October, 1704, the Cardinal reaffirmed Lucy Filippini's position as Directress of the Schools and designated her Superior General of the Institute. To eight of the former nuns, now members of the merged community, the Cardinal assigned official positions of responsibility. Thus he hoped to assuage their pain and gently remove natural obstacles caused by the merger. To the five Religious Teachers, who would live at the motherhouse with Lucy, he imposed no charge other than that of dedicating themselves totally to the school apostolate, either as qualified teachers in the Motherhouse School or as Religious Teachers-in-training.

Within the week, Cardinal Barbarigo began making improvements on the dilapidated motherhouse. The roof was repaired; two new classrooms were built, one on the first floor for summer use, the other on the second floor for the winter; additional windows were opened; walls and ceilings were painted. As security for future expansion, the Cardinal also purchased and reconditioned the house next door. That first year alone, he spent over one-thousand *scudi*.* When he finally obtained from the Township a piece of land behind the motherhouse, the Cardinal was relieved. Now the Teachers had a garden and an orchard to help support themselves.

At age twenty Lucy Filippini had anguished over her call to apostolic spirituality. She had feared that the School would reduce her prayer life to mere formality, to parceled time periods. Twelve grace-immersed years later, thirty-two-year-old Lucy, purified by suffering, living and breathing in the Divine Presence, basked in the light of God's Word and saw clearly the unity of all things. She suffered no dichotomy of self as she moved from prayer to work or from work to prayer. She had learned to find God in every situation and was continuing to discover God at the heart of all matter. She was growing as an apostolic-contemplative. Yet her union with God did not diminish her intuitive powers; did not insensitize her awareness of human needs; did not dull her practical nature or her business acumen; did not blind her understanding of

---

*A former monetary unit—gold or silver coin of Italy and Sicily—valued at about one dollar.

human nature. Rather, her growth in alertness and consciousness of everyone and everything around her kept pace with her increasing awareness of Christ's abiding spirit.

Only a woman steeped in God and in tune with the reality of His world can maintain an inner peace in time of persecution. Such a woman was Lucy. At first, everything seemed to be going well with the recently invested "nuns." Their relief in having enough to eat, decent accommodations and happy sister-companions stilled the latent discontent which had become so much a part of them. But, as the novelty of their security and physical well-being wore off, so did their suspended disquiet. And the leader in the campaign of hate and jealousy which broke open was no other than Chiara Felice Mereanzi, the very one who had opened the doors to the merger. With jaundiced eyes, Chiara observed the respect Lucy received from the Cardinal and other members of the hierarchy of the church. She resented the prudent measures employed by Lucy in her governing. Chiara interpreted Lucy's wisdom and gentle ruling as reproof of her own past administration. Capitalizing on the weaknesses of her former subjects, she initiated a campaign of slander, sowed seeds of contempt for the simple rules established by the Cardinal, and incited rebellion. Chiara's jealousy and pride hardened her towards Lucy, who patiently supported, corrected, exhorted and prayed for her conversion.

Kindly but firmly, Lucy called the former nuns to order. Unfortunately her plea for peace and good order fell on plugged ears and stony hearts. The tempest raged; the sounds of its violence escaped outside the convent walls. Lucy remained firm; she could not capitulate to the demands of these blinded women. To Lucy, following Christ meant embracing His poverty, imitating His obedience, living His chastity. Their life together required a common vision, a group united in His spirit. Never could Lucy condone the destruction of common life, nor could she close her eyes to the nuns' brazen disregard of the rules.

The town rumbled and shook under the furious, one-sided gossip spread by Chiara. The work of the School suffered. There was no way Lucy could defend herself without at the same time hurting the reputation of the former nuns. So she remained silent! Her Gethsamane continued! She feared the ruination of her Schools, the suppression of her infant Institute. Only her faithful Teachers supported and consoled her. She was not oblivious, however, to the derision her Teachers had to bear because of their steadfast loyalty to the rules and to her as their God-given superior.

Lucy's passionate love for the Crucified Christ provided the strength she needed to meet the daily attacks of rebellion and slander. She continued to serve her detractors, choosing the most humble offices in the house, reaching out to her tormentors with love and docility. Yet she continued to give the necessary orders, not in an authoritative manner, but in a prayerful tone. Never, however, did she condescend to allow human weakness to reign. Rather she sought to lead her community to higher planes as she continued to remain firm in her insistence of regular observance and, above all, of charity. Distraught by Lucy's strength of character, Chiara deliberately resolved to humiliate her by running away. After an unsuccessful attempt to solicit the help of Canon Bonaventura Verduzzi, who recognized her as a jealous woman, Chiara called upon her own sister and with her help planned the escape.

Chiara's act did inflict incalculable pain on Lucy, but not for the reasons Chiara intended; Lucy loved both her old friend and her Institute. She did not concern herself about the deeper shadow cast on her by the flight, making it seem that her rule was too severe and oppressing. What disturbed Lucy to the depths of her agonized soul was the offense against God and the Cardinal who had done so much for them. So much ingratitude caused her great sorrow. She bore the recriminations from Chiara Mereanzi's companions and friends outside the convent with a dignified silence. Lucy was very well aware of the suppositions, suspicions, and judgments this escape aroused, even in the good people, all of whom were ignorant of the undercurrents.

Cardinal Barbarigo had left for Rome on business only a few months after the merger; thus Lucy was deprived even of his advice and consolation.

To justify her actions, Chiara Mereanzi induced her former subjects to persist in their rebellion against common life; she encouraged them to follow her out so that more suspicion would be hurled against Lucy. After Chiara's departure, there was open defiance from the former nuns. They threatened to leave if Lucy did not relent. For Lucy there was no dilemma. She could not prevent the scandal of further departures by allowing the greater tragedy of permissiveness. As a free woman, she had only one choice: fidelity to her love-covenant with the Lord.

Two other nuns, Maria Inocente Ceci and Maria Rosalba Antonini, fled. Those who remained did so only because they had nowhere to go, so there was no relief for Lucy and her Teachers in the days ahead. The weight of the cross was becoming oppressive. The Body of Christ was being lacerated.

As Superior General and Directress of Schools, Lucy had the heavy responsibility of caring for all her Teachers scattered throughout the Diocese. Her infant Schools needed her undivided attention. Her young Teachers-in-training deserved a sun-filled environment where they could grow; they were the future. A clear-visioned Lucy considered the situation and weighed the alternatives.

Why should she remain here as superior? To be the occasion of other defections? Other scandals? Furthermore, the Schools at large required that she be free to administer to them! Her Schools would be suffocated before they could grow. She could not be bogged down with these internal problems. Could she be the cause of the unrest? Was something lacking in her? Perhaps her removal from the scene would bring peace. So why not write to the Cardinal—and resign from office? Then again that gnawing question: Was she doing her own will—or God's? What were her priorities? Why did she consider resignation the prudent solution? Was it because she could not bear the cross? Or was it because of her larger commitment to the whole institute?

Thus Lucy struggled through tortured, doubt-filled days. Her questions searched for one answer only—God's will! In the nakedness of her failure to uplift these poor women, Lucy gradually discerned God's will, her resignation as superior. With agonized determination, she wrote her letter of resignation, painfully aware of the sorrow she was inflicting on her beloved Cardinal. Fervently she prayed that he would understand and forgive her failure.

Before the Cardinal had departed from Montefiascone, the first rumblings of discontent had erupted at the monastery. It was with a heavy heart that he had left for Rome on business. Before leaving, he had counseled patience, but in the same breath he had insisted on firmness. He trusted that Lucy's example would convert the obstinate religious. Nevertheless, he realized that he had placed a heavy burden on Lucy's shoulders. His only hope was that she would win them over with her gentle manners and loving heart. Notwithstanding this, he must have recognized the fierce obstinacy of these women. He must have experienced definite tension, for long before he heard from Lucy he had already preoccupied himself with finding someone to replace her as Superior of the house. He was probably aware that her role there, in that particular situation, would rob her of the time she needed as Directress of Schools and Teachers.

Yet when the Cardinal, an incurable optimist, finally received Lucy's letter of resignation, he almost fainted from the pain. Needing to share his grief, he called for his confessor, Don Biagio Morani. Don Morani was a righteous man, a deeply contemplative ascetic, spiritual director of many souls. Among his counselees was a certain Catherine Comaschi, noted for her distinct piety. Morani described Miss Comaschi in glowing terms, confident that she would be an excellent replacement for Lucy.

Catherine had spent seven years in a cloistered community, but family problems had impeded her from taking final vows. Still intent on dedicating herself to God, she had under Morani's guidance continued to live a monastic life within the confines of her sister's home. She was, he concluded, an exemplary religious woman; perhaps she could direct these women. Morani's words revived the Cardinal's drooping spirits.

True to his nature, the Cardinal wanted immediate action.

51

Willingly Morani contacted Miss Comaschi, urging her to accept the Cardinal's invitation to assume the leadership of the new community. Cardinal Barbarigo added his personal plea both to her and to her family. Catherine accepted immediately, but it required strong persuasion to move the family, who regretted losing Catherine's capable help in their household. Finally, assured of Miss Comaschi's acceptance and the family's permission, the Cardinal returned to Montefiascone.

Immediately he visited Lucy to ascertain the particulars not contained in her brief letter. The full force of the tragic events which had occurred during his brief absence stunned him. Lucy's pain-filled eyes disturbed him; she had suffered beyond his expectation. Kindly he reassured her that a new superior would soon replace her. He recommended that in the future she devote all her energies to the Schools and Teachers-at-large.

Catherine Comaschi arrived in Montefiascone the 4th of February 1705, a brief four months after the solemn, canonical erection of the infant Institute. The very next morning the Cardinal called the community together and presented Catherine Comaschi to them as their new superior. When he asked them to promise obedience to her, several of the former nuns refused. The Cardinal firmly ordered them to collect their belongings and depart. A few did just that; the others, having nowhere to go, remained and reluctantly pledged obedience. Lucy, very much aware of the difficulties Miss Comaschi would face, offered her assistance in whatever way she could serve.

Lucy Filippini was now free to return to nearby St. Margaret, the former motherhouse of the Teachers in Montefiascone, to pursue her all-absorbing role as Directress of Schools and of the Teachers. But only Lucy left the monastery. The Teachers-in-training and those involved in the School there had to remain. Miss Comaschi would be the principal of that School and their superior. The monastery would continue to be the motherhouse and novitiate for the Religious Teachers.

Before the Cardinal left for Tarquinia that winter, he again exhorted Catherine to insist on obedience and adherence to community life, but he also warned her not to interfere with the School schedule. He was convinced from his own experience that work and prayer could and should blend into one. The Cardinal did not forsee any problem; more dissenters had left, reducing the possibility of further conflict. He left for Tarquinia at ease.

Catherine Comaschi gave her best self to the community, slowly imprinting upon it a strong, monastic character. She introduced the Divine Office, increased the hours of prayer, insisted on strict enclosure; all this she did in good faith. Catherine had no understanding of the school apostolate, nor of apostolic spirituality. The Teachers were frustrated by the rigorous schedule; they had no time to prepare their classes nor freedom to administer to the needs of the students and families they were serving. It was only natural that they seek advice from Lucy who was still Directress of Schools and Teachers.

Respectfully, Lucy approached Catherine to explain the needs and responsibilities of the Teachers and to beg her to be more understanding of their apostolate. She urged her to modify the schedule, reminding Catherine that this was an apostolic community, not a cloistered order. Catherine listened politely, but Lucy's words passed through her, unheeded.

To her Teachers Lucy advised prudence and respect; she urged them to remain calm and submissive. The Cardinal would rectify the situation when he returned from Tarquinia. All of her Teachers, except one, suffered patiently under Miss Comaschi. Angela Piccione, Lucy's compatriot and an orphan like herself, was the only rebellious Teacher. She could not and would not adjust to the rigid lifestyle imposed by Catherine Comaschi. When she demanded to join Lucy at St. Margaret's, Lucy could not grant her the permission; only the Cardinal had the right to transfer her. In fact, Lucy could not remove any of her Teachers from the Monastery School, nor could she change the schedule. She had power to do neither.

Angela's growing bitterness and open rebellion disturbed Lucy deeply. Together with Miss Comaschi, she tried to calm Angela. When Angela threatened to leave, they induced her to stay. The old nuns, however, welcomed the rebellious instigations. Again, hell broke loose. Now Catherine was experiencing what Lucy had suffered. Both wrote to the Cardinal independently. Lucy explained her teachers' complaints and begged him to take action; Catherine justified her manner of governing as obedience to his command that common life be vigorously observed. Furthermore, Catherine requested permission to solicit help from an old friend, Catherine Ridolfi from Castel Gandolfo. Miss Ridolfi, she said, was a deeply spiritual woman; with her aid, she could govern these women.

The Cardinal willingly gave Catherine Comaschi permission to call on Catherine Ridolfi; in fact, he wrote to her himself, begging her to go to Miss Comaschi's assistance. Then he wrote to Don Morani, asking him to leave Rome and take up residence in Montefiascone. It was urgent that he serve as Spiritual Director to the floundering community.

At the end of March 1705, Catherine Ridolfi and a companion she had invited to join her, Costanza Costanzi, arrived in Montefiascone. Catherine Comaschi, strengthened by the presence of her two assistants, enforced monastic living, demanding strict enclosure. The tempest boiled out of control.

Again and again Lucy wrote to the Cardinal, begging him to communicate with Catherine Comaschi, to caution her and counsel her regarding the School apostolate. However, so did the two Catherines write to the Cardinal, again and again, justifying their interpretation of community life, deploring the disobedience of the old nuns and of Angela Piccione. They admitted, however, that the other Teachers never lacked in respect or obedience.

The poor bewildered Cardinal was distraught. He had known Lucy a long time, loved her, and respected her. He read the terrible suffering in her letters. Every word reflected her sincerity. On the other hand, he hardly knew Catherine Comaschi. Yet, he held her in great esteem also, more so because she came so highly recommended by Don Morani for whom Barbarigo held great admiration. Miss Comaschi lived by her convictions which, he noted, were strictly monastic. The Cardinal felt impelled to cut short his stay in Tarquinia and return to Montefiascone. He had to see and hear for himself what the real problems were.

So on April 1, 1705 he returned to Montefiascone. First he heard Lucy, then Catherine. Sorrowfully he realized that both had just complaints. It was impossible for women of such diverse spiritualities to live under one *Rule*. But, he thought, it should not be impossible for them to live under one *roof*. His ever-active mind conceived a new plan, one he truly believed would work. He waited for Morani's arrival to test its worth with his scrutinizing mind. Morani arrived in Montefiascone on the 14th day of May in 1705. Considering himself unworthy to reside in the episcopal house, he took up residence in the poor hospice across from St. Margaret.

It was a relief for the Cardinal to have Morani available. To him he poured out his anguished grief about the monastery situation and especially about Angela Piccioni, whom he had sponsored from childhood. Orphaned at an early age, Angela had been brought to the orphanage in Tarquinia and had been educated there. Lucy had continued to care for her when she had decided to dedicate her life to God as a Teacher. He found it painful to look upon her face, now distorted with bitterness and anger. In her utter misery, she had spat out insults, even to him, who had always befriended her. He begged Morani to reach out to her. Morani promised to do so. Gradually Morani did break down the protective barriers Angela had built around herself. Finally, she did make a clean break from the evil eating away at her and did allow God to heal her. As extreme as she had been in her sin, so was she in her remorse. Not satisfied with asking forgiveness of Lucy and the Cardinal, she also made a public confession before her companions and begged forgiveness of them.

Angela never again turned her back on God. Her radical conversion soothed the wounds she had inflicted on her benefactors. Angela, however, was the only consolation; a belligerent atmosphere continued to prevail in the motherhouse.

Cardinal Barbarigo was relentless in his search to save his new found institute, even if it meant making drastic changes. It wasn't long before the plan brewing in the Cardinal's mind took definite form. To Morani the Cardinal confided the design of the new community step by step.

The Cardinal intended to erect a new congregation which would consist of two branches. The first he would call "Congregation of Divine Love," the other "the Banquet of the Celestial Spouse." In the first would be admitted women called to monastic life who would take vows and follow a rigorous prayer life. These women would enjoy both active and passive voice and would be eligible for all offices of authority within the congregation. The Pre-elects would lead the lay women in mental prayer and conduct spiritual exercises for the first communicants. There were to be no more than thirteen of these Pre-elects at one time in one house. Into "The Banquet of the Celestial Spouse" would be admitted the Teachers, or the Elects. At first the Cardinal had considered giving this second group both the active and passive voice. But it was quite obvious that Catherine Comaschi and Don Morani had persuaded the Cardinal to take away both. Thus all directive offices of government would be denied to the Teachers. Even the formation of new Teachers would be in the hands of the Pre-elects. Intuitively Lucy recognized the dangers inherent in the new plan, especially under the leadership of Don Morani and Catherine Comaschi, who had no understanding of or sympathy for the School apostolate.

Firmly believing he had found the solution to the problem, the Cardinal presented the plan to Lucy and her Teachers, leaving them free to accept or reject the invitation to join. Lucy was grateful for this freedom.

The Cardinal was confident that Lucy and her Teachers would embrace the new congregation. Lucy's analytical mind, however, enlightened by the gift of wisdom and intuition, evaluated the implications of the proposal carefully: What would happen, she thought, after the death of the Cardinal? Would her group be evicted from the congregation, or would it be impeded from carrying on its apostolate? And what vehicle of communication was open to them? None! They had no voice whatsoever in chapter decisions, having been denied both active and passive voice in the government of the congregation!

56

Her new Teachers concerned her deeply. Their formation would be in the hands of the Pre-elects, whose understanding of contemplatives-in-action was nil. How could they prepare novices for an apostolic-contemplative life?

Her thoughts traveled to her Teachers scattered throughout the diocese. Could her Teaching Community possibly adjust its present lifestyle to the one imposed by the newly formulated constitution? Her Teachers carried their cloister within their hearts; they were contemplatives-in-action, servants of God's people.

If she accepted the invitation to join, would not her Schools gradually be snuffed out?

Lucy's vision, illumined by the light of God's abiding Word within her, revealed His will for her. Her answer to the Cardinal's invitation had to be "no." Lucy could not compromise the existence of her Schools and the continuation of her social apostolate, so desperately needed to restore the Christian family.

Thus it was that Lucy Filippini's wisdom and strength of purpose rescued the community from destruction. Thus it was that Lucy's judicious "no" strengthened the roots of the wind-shaken community and gave it stability. *Thus it was that Lucy became Foundress of the Religious Teachers Filippini.*

7

Instilling a Sense of Mission

> *Go into the whole world*
> *and proclaim the good*
> *news to all creation.*
> —Luke 16:15

Lucy FILIPPINI'S faith-filled "no" to the Cardinal confirmed her steadfast "yes" to God. A paradox of love! A dying and a being born. Violent, overflowing pain invaded her whole being. She had wounded her beloved friend and spiritual father—her benefactor. She longed to comfort him. She yearned to reassure him that her *negative* response was most profoundly *affirmative,* most in harmony with his initial goal. She desired to console him as a mother does a son who cannot foresee imminent peril.

In the anguish of his shattered hope, the Cardinal must have publicly expressed his disappointment. The news of his displeasure spread rapidly. Lucy, the townsmen buzzed, had lost favor with the Cardinal.

The School in Montefiascone felt the impact; the Religious Teachers suffered; Lucy was in a quandary!

Her position as Superior General of the Religious Teachers was untenable. She would not, at this crucial moment in the life of the Schools, become a bridle to their existence. Painfully serene, Lucy accepted the inevitable. She had no choice but to ask the Cardinal to commit her position to another. And in order to spare him further agony, she would seek admission into Rose Venerini's Schools. Her departure from the scene would reduce the tension caused by the rumor.

Immediately, Lucy wrote a letter to this effect, both to Father

58

Martinelli and to Rose Venerini. Both welcomed the news; Lucy would be a blessing among them. Now, it would be necessary to approach Cardinal Barbarigo for his permission.

But, before Lucy could carry out her resolve, the Cardinal summoned her to the episcopal residence. The gossip had reached his ears also. The Cardinal loved and esteemed Lucy; moreover, he recognized her worth. At this point in time, the Schools would crumble without her leadership.

Humbly, the Cardinal reaffirmed his faith and trust in her and declared his intention to make this statement public. What else, he pleaded, could he do to reassure the people of his unbroken confidence in her? What more could he do for her? What gift could he bestow on her?

Lucy, her heart aflame with love for God and with deep admiration for the Cardinal asked but one favor—that the Cardinal support her in the quest for souls.

Lucy's simplicity and humility edified the good Cardinal.

At his soft request to continue as Superior General, Lucy yielded. Her fidelity to the "yes" was and would ever be her joy and her crucifixion.

Lucy Filippini and her Teachers in Montefiascone delighted in the warm companionship of their reunited religious family. The Teachers, returned from the monastery, voiced their thanksgiving in song and prayer. They were among their own. The Teachers at St. Margaret welcomed them home. Their circle was complete now. They had suffered much, separately and collectively. In their shared sufferings, the bond of their friendship had been strengthened.

The Teachers looked upon Lucy and read her eyes. There they saw what she had made of her sorrows. Her face reflected joy, peace, and confidence. They noted, however, the burning pain which would live in the corner of her being forever. They knew that in her steadfast fidelity to Christ, Lucy would ever carry His cross, even unto death. When she spoke to them of Christ's passion and death, her whole being cried out to them. She became ecstatic, unable to contain her broken tears of compassion and boundless love. She had tasted the bittersweet joy of wounded pain in His Name.

The Religious Teachers outside of Montefiascone longed for a reunion. They yearned to hear Lucy; her words always renewed them. They wanted to be strengthened in the warmth of her love. Lucy sensed the desire of her Teachers, which was no less her own. They needed one another.

The Montefiascone Teachers joined Lucy in planning the reunion. It would be a celebration of praise and thanksgiving, of reconciliation. It would be a time for the re-creation of each one for everyone. It would be a time to renew and cement friendships. It would be a time to rediscover and reaffirm their individual and united commitment to serve God as contemplatives-in-action, commissioned to restore the Christian family through the School and social apostolate.

Everyone joined in the preparations for the missionaries' homecoming. They cleaned house, fixed beds, baked, decorated the refectory, prepared the entertainment, adorned the altar with flowers. It was a blessed time of fraternal sharing and healing.

The Teachers scattered here and there in the small towns around Lake Bolsena, as well as those in Tarquinia, were jubilant. They were going home to Lucy in Montefiascone for a celebration!

Poignant gladness converged into harmonious buzzing as the Religious Teachers greeted each other. Happy tears blessed their joy as they embraced their beloved Lucy. Everyone talked at once; radiant voices dispelled the lingering darkness of the past seven months. Happiness permeated every nook and corner of that house; Lucy basked in the light of their rejoicing.

After a gloriously sung liturgy, the Teachers enjoyed a delicious meal prepared and served by the youngest Teachers. Just before the dessert was served, Lucy stood to address her religious family. Her voice was husky with emotion as she thanked God for them; they were precious to her—each and everyone.

Her eyes bright with love, Lucy spoke in praise of their beloved benefactor and spiritual father, Cardinal Marc Anthony Barbarigo. He was, she acclaimed, a man on fire with love for God and

His Church. Lucy affirmed her admiration for his new congregation and blessed the Teachers who had affiliated themselves with it. She exhorted the Teachers to be unwavering in their gratitude to the Cardinal. Moreover, they should often express their gratitude to him. Lucy also commended Catherine Comaschi for her deep spirituality.

Then her voice, strong with the confidence of a woman tuned in to His voice, proclaimed her own calling—hers and theirs. They were called to teach, to evangelize, to preach. *Their* inner vision of the new Jerusalem was *their* cloister.

Her voice pierced their hearts, reanimated their zeal. A boundless energy enlightened their minds and moved their wills; they shared her sense of mission fully.

Lucy stated her readiness to resume her former responsibilities, both to the Schools and to the Cardinal. She would continue to be the Cardinal's precursor on his pastoral visits. She would begin her School visitations very soon.

She ended her talk as she always did, tenderly expressing her love and concern for each and every one. She urged them to keep her informed concerning their needs, their problems, and their successes.

During the dessert, the Teachers began to taste the sadness of their departure. Yet their hearts were luminous with hope and secure in their experienced fraternal union. Lucy had a way of dispelling all darkness, a way of making all things new and beautiful and joy-filled.

The healing process had begun. Her Teachers would bring back to their local communities their restored hope and deep-found peace. However, it would be Lucy's responsibility to confirm their message. Carefully Lucy planned her itinerary, taking into consideration where the need was greatest. Before leaving Montefiascone, several of the principals had confided their problems to her. They had asked her to come soon.

Lucy had established a more or less flexible pattern for her School visitations. After her customary visit to the church, Lucy usually met with the women to give them meditation. In the classroom observation which followed, Lucy noted carefully the rapport between Teacher and girls:

Was the Teacher transferring her sense of mission to the girls? Were they living the Christian message of love and service? Was the Teacher faithful to the method given them by Cardinal Barbarigo? Did the Teacher recognize and provide for individual differences? Was the Teacher compassionate . . . lovingly firm . . . well-prepared . . . Christ immersed?

The School would be as effective as the spirit which ruled!

Very often, Lucy took over the classes. Her gift of perception and her keen understanding of children rendered her powerful. Her message lifted their self-worth, elevated their concept of womanhood. Though different from men, they were nevertheless equally powerful, equally responsible members of society. In fact, the very sanctity of the home depended largely on them! In this manner did Lucy speak to the hearts of the girls.

After school, Lucy, in the company of another Teacher or student, visited the sick and dying of the parish. She never went empty-handed—the sick appreciated her gifts of fruit, cheese, or wine. They were comforted by her concern and compassion. Her visits were like a balm, a breath of hope.

In the evening the rel!gous family gathered around Lucy. The Teachers were eager to hear news of the other Schools, of their sister-Teachers, happy to listen to her inspiring words.

She exhorted them to give alms. Deny no one, she would say, because it is charity which maintains the Schools. She cautioned them to respect the poor. If they noticed that a person of high rank was in need and ashamed to seek alms, they should take it upon themselves to seek help for him from wealthier persons. (Lucy knew how to solicit large sums which she used to help the embarrassed poor.)

Poverty, she would say to them, binds us to one another. Just as Jesus took on the poverty of manhood to live among us, so her Teachers should embrace poverty. In this manner they would infuse divine life into the congregation. The beginning of all laxity, she warned them, was the failure to maintain the poverty of Christ in the Institute. She instructed them to make poverty indivisible from the community so that, like the apostles, they would be free from earthly baggage and thus be ready and prompt to follow Jesus.

However Lucy did not recommend or even advise squalor or habitual privations, nor exterior signs of indigence. Rather, in imitation of Christ's life in Nazareth, she wisely counseled that their exterior life be common rather than outstandingly rigid. She stressed the spirit of perpetual apostolic poverty. Lucy went so far as to say that once the Schools were provided for, the Teachers were to be cautious about accepting wills and testaments.

She exhorted her Teachers to refrain from complaining, but rather to be happy when they lacked even the necessities of life. Christ, during His public life, had no place He could call His own, nowhere to rest His tired Body. The greatest recompense of poverty, she said, would be their encounter with Christ. Her Teachers witnessed the Living Word in Lucy; she was what she preached.

Lucy's poverty was tranquil. She expected little or nothing from anyone. Yet, whatever anyone gave her she accepted gratefully; she lived only by alms. Interiorly naked, Lucy considered nothing hers by right.

Lucy's rare gift of discernment enabled her to read the unspoken concerns of her Religious-Teachers even before they confided them to her. The Teachers did not find it difficult to approach Lucy for advice or for help in time of need. Whether that need was financial, physical, or spiritual made no difference.

Once a Teacher, distraught to tears, came to Lucy. She needed financial help for personal reasons. Moved to compassion, Lucy, having no money with her, offered her a gold cross which her sister Elizabeth had given her. She gave the Teacher permission to sell the cross and use the funds according to her need.

Whenever a Teacher fell ill, Lucy went to her immediately, no matter what the inconvenience. She cared for her with the tender love of a mother; she did not leave until the Teacher was well again. Each Teacher without exception experienced Lucy's individual concern for her. Many times the Teachers tried to hide their illnesses. Their zeal for God's work spurred them on to heroic acts of self-denial.

One day Lucy noted the pallid face and forced smile of one of her Teachers. The young religious had been suffering from dysentery and persistent headaches, yet she had never uttered a complaint. Immediately Lucy made arrangements to take her to the doctor in Viterbo. Twice she accompanied her there. She spared no expenses when a Teacher's health was at stake. Nor did she hesitate to adjust the rule to meet the particular needs of her Teachers. Solicitously, Lucy ordered the sick Teacher to take broth every day, including days of abstinence, encouraged her to rest later in the morning, told her to leave during the hour of prayer in order to take refreshment. Yet Lucy never tolerated any laxity in the observance of common life.

Lucy Filippini was a woman, a real woman—compassionate, courageous, self-giving. Lucy Filippini was a free woman, detached from self-interest, tireless in her service to God and man.

In all kinds of weather Lucy traveled to her Schools. Very often she lost her way and was compelled to travel through thorns and briars. There were no paved roads leading to the small towns; nor were there sign posts giving directions. Many times Lucy arrived at her destination, her clothes torn and tattered.

The winding, wooded roads of those days harbored untold perils. But Lucy never feared; in her boundless faith she walked with God.

Lucy either walked from one School to the other or traveled by donkey. Occasionally Cardinal Barbarigo gave her the use of his carriage. Once, when Lucy and a companion were traveling to Tessennano on a donkey, a furious thunder and lightning storm broke. At this point, they were approaching the open fields of Arlena. The frightened donkey refused to move on. Lucy's companion burst into tears, convinced death was imminent. With lively faith, Lucy raised her eyes to God and prayed the psalm, "Praise the Lord, from the heavens" (Psalm 148). Instantly, the clouds dissipated, the lightning and thunder ceased.

On another occasion Lucy set out to inspect a farm belonging to one of the Schools. Suddenly a wild dog appeared from nowhere, and sprang like a tiger upon her. Throwing her to the ground, the dog jumped on her, determined to tear her apart. Again Lucy's faith saved her. "Jesus and Mary, help me!" was her trusting plea. Each time the dog's teeth touched her flesh, his jaws locked. He could only tatter her clothes to shreds! Lucy remained in the thralls of the wild animal for some time. Finally the noise of a gathering crowd frightened away the beast. Serenely Lucy picked herself up, praising God for the mercy He had shown her.

One day Lucy and a companion were again traveling by donkey. The Paglia River, which they had to cross, was dangerously high and rapid. In fact, it had just overturned a laden donkey. Her companion feared the same fate would be theirs. With confidence, Lucy told her not to fear; the sign of the cross would be their bridge. They did cross safely, to the astonishment of a disbelieving bystander.

Thirteen years had elapsed since the opening of the first Schools. A spirited, courageous, far-sighted, practical, faithful Lucy Filippini continuously breathed life into her struggling Schools. Her breath was that of a woman whose very existence exhaled love, a love born of faith. Whatever Lucy did for the least of her people she did for Him Whom she knew lived in them.

Gratefully Lucy recognized the regenerated offspring of the Schools. A new *woman* was in procress—a woman who knew her self-worth, who recognized her powerful place in society, who was equipped to wage a quiet revolution grounded on the Beatitudes.

In Latera, the women were beginning to discover happiness without the aid of wine. In Gradoli, the women were using their gift of speech to spread the good news of Christ. In Piansano, their love of beauty took on a new depth. Everywhere music filled the air as usual, but with songs learned in the Schools. Everywhere more and more families worshipped together every Sunday and prayed together every day.

Christianity was taking on a deeper meaning; it was becoming a way of life. Not that it had become easier to follow Christ; to walk in His footsteps would never be easy. But her Schools were graduating strong women who were not afraid to be different, who were not fearful of the daily crosses life presented. Lucy's Schools were begetting liberated women whose faith-filled trust in Divine Providence freed them from needless anxieties.

8

Losing a Father

> *When a work is of God, that*
> *same God is bound to maintain*
> *it.*
> —Lucy Filippini

CARDINAL BARBARIGO'S yearly pastoral reports document
for posterity the tremendous impact of Lucy Filippini's Schools on
the eighteenth-century Italian woman. In his 1694 official report to
Rome, the Cardinal's praise for the Schools' contribution to the
spiritual growth of his diocese was exuberant. In 1699 his
description of the Teaching Community and their influence on the
people spoke his sincere gratitude. "Their exemplary lives," he
declared, "marked by extraordinary piety, modesty, and generosity
are bearing much fruit." After his formal visitation of the School
in Montefiascone in 1704, he wrote that the students were very well
instructed, that the School was like a sanctuary where joy and
Christian charity prevailed, that the girls were filled with apostolic
fervor.

Gratitude for Lucy Filippini and her Teaching Community made
up the major portion of every report the Cardinal wrote from 1692
to 1706. Humbly he admitted that whatever progress had been
made toward the restoration of the family to Christ could be at-
tributed in great part to the Schools.

By means of the pastoral visitations, the Cardinal knew each
Teacher personally, had direct contact with the students and
women who attended the workshops, was acquainted with every
pastor and knew firsthand the spiritual, moral, and financial status
of the parish.

Cardinal Barbarigo's yearly parish visitations were an integral part of his episcopacy. Through these pastoral visits he discovered budding abuses, fathomed the "why" of persistent problems, determined the steps he had to take in each instance.

From the very beginning it was the Cardinal's generosity and simplicity which had captivated the hearts of his people. His artless approach to the problems and needs of his parishoners revealed his humility and sincerity. He was not an opportunist; he had no political ambitions, no desire for honors or riches. He had only one burning ambition, to restore the Kingdom of God in his diocese and everywhere.

Every year he commissioned two or more vigorous missionaries to conduct a five-week mission in preparation for his visit to the parish. The preachers made themselves available to the people, listened to their complaints, heard their pleas for help, promised to mediate for them, encouraged them to receive the sacraments. They took mental notes of the people's physical needs, of the prevalent problems and the possible causes. Their observations facilitated the Cardinal's pastoral activity.

Lucy Filippini also preceded the Cardinal. She conducted a ten-day spiritual retreat for women. Recognizing Lucy as their most powerful mediator with the Cardinal, the women exposed their difficulties to her, trustingly and hopefully. Lucy's sharp mind, inspired by the power of discernment, pierced the symptoms and uncovered the underlying causes of the problems confided to her by the women. Her open-hearted report to the Cardinal prepared him for whatever action he had to take.

The Cardinal always arrived several days before the end of the five-week mission. After meeting with the mission fathers and Lucy, he plunged into his work. A variety of liturgical functions filled his morning up to noon hour. While his priests dined, the Cardinal, who fasted until supper, received those people who wished to see him for whatever reason. He gave his undivided attention to each one and whenever feasible bestowed the favor asked.

After the interviews, the Cardinal spoke to the school children assembled in the church. In their presence all fatigue vanished. In them rested tomorrow's society. The success of his reform movement, he firmly believed, depended not only on how well they were educated but also on how convinced they were of their sacred mission in life *as Christian women.*

But of course he expected them to know the truths of the faith. So he began his hour with them by questioning them, keeping in mind their respective ages and the number of years they had attended school. To encourage them in their studies, he rewarded them with prizes he always carried in his vast pockets.

He commissioned them to be teachers in their own homes, to be missionaries in their neighborhoods. He dared them to witness to Christ's presence in their world. His words inspired them; they sensed the tremendous importance of their mission. The School was the "apple of his eyes." Woe to anyone who insulted or disturbed one of his Teachers or students. He stopped at nothing to defend their honor.

One day, a Teacher and her class were returning to school from Mass. On the way, they met a group of boys playing bocce. One of the boys was the son of the governor and confident that his wealth and position gave him superiority and the right to do as he pleased. He approached one of the girls and wiped his mud-spattered ball on her apron. He paid dearly for the insult. The Cardinal had him imprisoned, and the family was asked to move to another town.

Also highly important to the Cardinal were the adult classes for women taught by one of the Teachers, or by Lucy whenever she was in town. Immediately after his visit with the girls, the Cardinal dropped in to see the women whose classes were usually filled to capacity. With the passing of years, the number of alumnae in the adult classes had increased; their presence rejuvenated the Cardinal. These were the women who were restoring Christ to society.

His message to the women had become an old familiar tune! Women were the backbone of society; they determined the health or sickness of the next generation. They were the heart and soul of the Christian family. His words strengthened their sense of self-worth and inspired them to live the Christian faith despite any ridicule hurled against them.

At the end of the day, after classes were dismissed, the Cardinal met with his Religious Teachers. In fact, he visited them every day during his stay in town. The Teachers' filial love for him touched him deeply; his love for them was also profound.

For their welfare, he willingly incurred large debts. Generously, he provided for them. Every year he gave each Teacher eighteen *scudi* and two pairs of shoes, every two years—a new habit. Very often, but especially on feast days, he provided delicacies for their table.

For the Teachers' spiritual well-being, the Cardinal spared no expense. Wherever there were Schools, he assigned holy and energetic priests. The spiritual life of his Teachers held first place in the Cardinal's daily activities. Therefore, despite his busy schedule, he always found time to instruct them, to spend time with them. He exhorted them to be, what their title named them—*Holy Teachers*. "My Teachers," he used to say, "must be like clouds laden with water which they must rain upon the souls of the entire diocese."

He was their confessor and spiritual director. Every year he invited them to come together and rest awhile in the Lord. For this reason they gathered in Montefiascone for ten days of spiritual retreat preached by Father Domenic Longobardi or another Pious Father whose chief responsibility was to minister to the needs of the Teachers and the Schools. The Cardinal, however, always gave several of the meditations and instructions, himself. In fact, he rarely missed an opportunity to speak to them whenever the community-at-large came together. On every occasion, he reviewed the teaching method he had imposed upon them. He insisted, however, that a Teacher was as *effective* as her *attitudes* were Christian. What they were becoming *in* and *with* Christ was what the girls would learn *of Christ*.

The awesomeness of their responsibility struck them anew whenever the Cardinal or Lucy spoke to them. How often was the spirit of those first Teachers kindled and rekindled by the co-founders! How clearly they perceived the sacredness of their apostolate. It was in the light of their founders' wisdom that the embryonic community of Teachers grew into maturity.

The year 1706 marked the fourteenth anniversary of the founding of the first School in Montefiascone, the twenty-eighth anniversary of the Cardinal's consecration as bishop, and the eighteenth anniversary of his episcopate in Montefiascone. In all those eighteen years the Cardinal had never interrupted his yearly pastoral visits. Nor did he this year, despite his utter exhaustion.

But before planning his itinerary, he called for Lucy, whose first-hand information concerning the spiritual and financial conditions in the Schools was invaluable to him. Often her keen observations and insights determined where the Cardinal went first or where he stayed longest.

On this particular occasion, the Cardinal confided to Lucy the plan he had conceived to insure the Schools' financial security. He conceded, however, that it would be a few years before the fund he had set aside for the Schools could produce profit. It was his dream to leave the Schools well-provided-for. But, he added quietly, if it were God's will that he die before his dream were actualized, he trusted that Divine Providence would not fail to intervene. Having shared his financial plan for the welfare of the Schools, the Cardinal sat back and listened to Lucy whose insights he valued. Without exaggerating the current problems, Lucy described the needs of that year—1706:

Grotte di Castro required attention immediately. The last earthquake had created havoc.

The School in Marta was low on funds. Sadly the Cardinal and Lucy paused to reflect on Marta. Conversion was slow there. That fishing town was obstinate in its immorality. The Cardinal's and Lucy's anguish was one as they prayed for the people of Marta. Later that year Lucy would recall this dialogue concerning Marta. (A few hours before his death, the Cardinal expressed his undying concern for his suffering Teachers assigned in Marta. In those last final hours he ordered that silk for their habits, plus wine and food, be sent immediately to the Teachers there.)

Having charted the order of his visits, the Cardinal returned home to begin the first phase of his pastoral visitations, which consisted of several weeks of concentrated private prayer and rigorous fasting.

As was customary, Lucy went ahead of the Cardinal to prepare the way for his visitation.

On April 29th, the Cardinal visited Marta; Valentano on the 30th . . . Latera on the 1st of May . . . Gradoli, the 2nd . . . St. Lorenzo, the 4th . . . Celleno, the 9th . . . back to Montefiascone, the 10th. Lucy begged him to rest during this interval; he needed it badly. Her affectionate concern touched the Cardinal, but it did not influence him. On May 20th, he returned to the Lake Bolsena region to visit Grotte di Castro.

Lucy's heart bled with grief during those crowded days. She noted the increasing pallor of his skin, the trembling hands, the hoarse voice. When he bade farewell to the people of Grotte lovingly gathered around him, Lucy's strong premonition told her the worst. He was giving these people, who had been most responsive to him, his last blessing.

It was May 21, 1706, the vigil of Pentecost. Both the Cardinal and Lucy were returning home to Montefiascone. With trembling poignancy, Lucy remembered that first carriage ride with the Cardinal across the marshlands from Tarquinia to Montefiascone. So much had transpired since that July of 1688.

She could not conceive of a future without his benevolent presence. Yet she knew, deep within her, that he would be ever-present. A love like his lived forever—in the strength he had supplied, in the common vision they had shared, in the instructions he had given, in the Schools he had founded, in the spirituality he had inspired, in the human concern he had manifested. Their lives were everlastingly interwoven—his and hers, his and the Institute's. With these reflections, Lucy endeavored to brace herself for the inevitable.

A totally exhausted Cardinal, burning with fever, arrived at his episcopal residence that 21st day of May. Hiding his condition from his fellow priests, he attended first Vespers at the Cathedral that evening. That night the fever mounted so high that nothing could warm him. Nevertheless, the next morning he prayed the Divine Office on his knees, as was his custom. At the appointed hour, he went to the Cathedral to celebrate the Pontifical High

Mass for the feast of Pentecost, the birthday of the Church. His homily was short but fiery; his words touched the people to the very depths of their being. Finally, he turned to his congregation and gave them what was to be his last blessing.

Lucy was there, of course. Spent with emotion, she received that blessing also. She knew it was the last time she would see him alive. Quietly, she bowed her head. It was God's will; again, she pronounced her *"yes"* to Him.

After the Mass, the Cardinal could no longer conceal his malady. Humbly he yielded to the priests who insisted that he go to bed. That evening he had to forego Vespers despite his ardent desire to attend.

Realizing that this sickness was unto death, the Cardinal requested that Masses be offered for him in all of the principal churches of the diocese. He was going Home to his Father; he wanted to be prepared. He called for his confessor, Don Biagio Morani. With great compunction, he made a general confession of all the offenses he had committed during his lifetime. He proclaimed his undying love for God and His Church. Very simply he thanked God for all the graces bestowed on him; he thanked Him especially for his priesthood. He entrusted his works and above all, his dear daughters, the Religious Teachers, into the Hands of Divine Providence.

They were the last words he spoke. His mind, however, remained lucid to the end. As he received the last rites of the Church, his lips formed the words of the prayers silently. His eyes betrayed his longing to see the God he had served so well for sixty-six years.

Cardinal Marc Antonio Barbarigo breathed his last on May 26, 1706. It was the feast of St. Philip Neri to whom he had been devoted all his life.

Everyone mourned him. He had been all things to all people. With his educational institutions, he had dissipated ignorance. He had befriended the poor; he had challenged the rich to share their wealth. He had improved living conditions; he had begun the movement to restore the family to Christ.

Everyone wanted something to remember him by: a strand of

hair, a fragment of clothing, a rosary he had touched—anything. Despite the precautions taken, many did succeed in securing a "relic" of their esteemed father and friend.

His funeral gave testimony to the magnanimity of his life. Bishops, priests, rich and poor, those from his diocese and outside of it attended the services. They came to pay their last respects to a man who had never failed to respect others.

Pope Clement XI, in a public consistory held later that year, openly expressed his grief. He proposed Cardinal Barbarigo as a worthy model to the College of Cardinals. Furthermore, he asked all bishops to pattern their pastoral visitations on the Cardinal's.

Lucy Filippini was alone! She felt the stark reality of her position. A gamut of emotions raced through her—fear, trust, loneliness, faith, quiet sorrow, peaceful acceptance. Turning to the Cardinal, who no longer required space or time to listen to her pleas, she entrusted "their" work to his mediation. In her heart she heard his response. "Pick up your cross and follow Him. *In your 'yes' to Him is your strength.*"

When the Cardinal's last will was probated and made public, Lucy recalled his often-expressed desire to leave them well provided for. She was not surprised, therefore, when she heard that he had named the Schools sole heir to his entire fortune. In his will he stipulated that immediately upon his death, the entire substance that made up his estate should be sold and converted into money and securities. Said money and securities were to be placed into a School Fund for the Girls' Schools. From the interest of the deposited sum, the Schools of his diocese would be permanently maintained.

To his bishop-successors he recommended that the Teaching Institute and Schools be protected and maintained in flourishing condition.

The administration of the funds he placed in the hands of the first two dignitaries of the Cathedral. These two men, in dialogue with the economic board of the Seminary, were to dispense the monies to the Schools and to the Teachers as needed.

Lucy had administered the funds while the Cardinal was alive.

The Cardinal had recognized her business acumen but had thought it unique to Lucy. He doubted the business capability of ordinary women. His will expressed that innate fear. This stipulation was to become the heaviest beam on Lucy's cross.

Ordinarily, for the upkeep of the Schools and Teachers, the Cardinal had spent a minimum of 1,500 *scudi* yearly. This sum did not include the expenses of the spiritual exercises. The minimum required to maintain the Schools alone was at least 840 *scudi*; this provided only for the bare necessities.

The last few years had decreased the Cardinal's financial reserves drastically. He had had to borrow money to meet not only the extraordinary expenses but also the current, ordinary ones. He had remodeled St. Clare's Monastery. An epidemic in Tarquinia had attacked the Teachers and orphans; those bills had been astronomical. He owed long overdue pensions to several of his retired priests. To meet these emergencies, the Cardinal had borrowed money. In the last two years his expenses had exceeded his revenues.

But there was another reason for the strait circumstances. The Cardinal could say "no" to no one. When Monsignor Bernardino Recchi, during his apostolic visitation, had warned the Cardinal to spend more cautiously, the Cardinal had responded, "It is a shame for a merchant to die penniless and full of debts, but what a glory for a bishop to die without even a pair of breeches."

That just about happened. When the Cardinal's estate was liquidated, there remained no more than six hundred *scudi*. The Schools were to be maintained on the yearly interest of thirty *scudi*. Lucy had inherited a cross! And for awhile she had to carry it without human support. Everywhere she turned, she met pessimism. The townspeople hopelessly mourned the death of their Schools. They refused to be resigned. The good people dreaded a return to what used to be before the Schools. Pastors were overwhelmed with anxiety; in no way could they support the Schools.

Lucy was besieged on all sides. What was going to happen to the Teachers? To the Schools? Was there nothing she could do to save them?

God was her only strength, and to Him Lucy Filippini turned. Only He could supply the courage she needed! Only He could guide her. Lucy prayed without ceasing, day and night. She fasted. Her constant prayer was that His will be done. If the Schools were His will, He had to protect them. He had to show her the way.

Her complete abandonment to His will gave her the strength to rise from her knees enlightened and empowered to take action.

She resolved to appeal to Pope Clement XI! She chose Father Domenic Longobardi as mediator. Lucy knew that Clement XI held Father Longobardi in great esteem for the good he was doing throughout Italy. Both the Pope and Father Longobardi recognized the worth of the Schools. The Pope had been well informed by the Cardinal himself. In fact, the Pope, she recalled, had often asked the Cardinal to open a School in Rome. Respectfully the Cardinal had voiced his refusal; he had wanted the Schools to be firmly rooted in his own diocese first. He would then gladly open Schools in Rome and everywhere in the world, he had promised. The Pope had smiled and had agreed to wait. Lucy remembered the Cardinal's facial expression as he had recounted the story to her.

As for Father Longobardi, he was well-acquainted with the work of the Schools on a first-hand basis. Very often it was he who gave the Community the yearly retreats; very often it was he who had preceded the Cardinal on his pastoral visitations. Lucy trusted him with her case.

When Lucy contacted Father Longobardi, he readily agreed to go to Clement XI, confident that all would go well. Lucy had chosen her advocate wisely.

Without hesitation Clement XI consented to do everything in his power to save the Schools. The Pope acted immediately. On June 12th, less than a month after the Cardinal's death, the Schools and Teachers were again provided for by the explicit orders of Clement XI. All bills were assumed by the papal treasury and would continue to be until the arrival of the new bishop late that December.

To be better informed about the actual state of affairs, the Pope sent his apostolic visitator, Monsignor Bernardino Recchi, to investigate every phase of the work.

Monsignor Recchi's report extolled the work of the Schools, praised the dedication of the Religious Teachers, and commended Lucy Filippini, whose leadership gave heart and dynamic direction to the growing Institute.

Monsignor's financial report, however, went beyond the tangible needs, which were indeed very evident. With clarity of expression, he described the late Cardinal's school attendance policy. To encourage the poor to send their daughters to School, the Cardinal had actually provided hemp for the girls' dowries at his own expense. He did this so that the parents would have no excuse to keep their daughters home. The Cardinal had maintained that while the girls converted the raw material to finery they were simultaneously drinking in the truths of the faith and learning how to live as Christian women. In the mind of the late Cardinal, the benefits derived more than compensated for the expenses incurred.

For the present, Monsignor commented, it was mandatory that this policy be kept—or the poor would once again be lost. The parents would be constrained to keep their girls home to earn money for their dowries.

Moreover, both Father Longobardi and Monsignor Recchi cautioned, the Cardinal's successor had to be someone who would continue to support the Schools, in principle and in fact.

Clement XI heard the pleas bearing down upon him from all sides. Though he was already maintaining the Schools, he had to do more. With largess of heart, he ruled that all episcopal stipends accrued since the Cardinal's death be kept in the diocese and used to pay bills owed by the Cardinal. Furthermore, he ordered that diocesan taxes owed to the Vatican be reduced. Lovingly the good Pope promised to select a bishop attuned to education and committed to the poor.

The distressed populace expressed their relief in jubilant song; the pastors sighed contentedly. The girls celebrated their restored security. The Teachers, at one with Lucy, were transported with joy. Lucy remembered her Cardinal's strong faith-filled words, "Divine Providence will never fail to intervene."

9

Walking Alone

> *Willingly I accept this little*
> *suffering from the Hands of*
> *God. I would even place myself*
> *on the cross and let myself be*
> *crucified for Jesus Christ, as He*
> *so willingly did for me, for it is*
> *not just that the bride enjoys*
> *herself while her Beloved suffers*
> *pain and torment.''*
> —Lucy Filippini

FOR SEVEN MONTHS—from May to December 1706—thirty-four-year-old Lucy Filippini governed her vulnerable Institute, alone. Canon Luca Corneli and Canon Alessandro Mazzinelli, the two dignitaries into whose hands the Cardinal had entrusted the financial administration of the congregation, quietly delegated their assigned role to Lucy. Her prudent handling of money was no secret to them. In her they saw the prosaic and mystical sensitively fused.

But Lucy had enemies also, and she knew it. Her intelligence pierced the reality of facts and events; her senses discerned what was happening around her. She was alive to the envy and jealousy of some of the clergy. They bristled over the Cardinal's will; they resented the Pope's concern for the Schools. Lucy was very much aware of the forces working against her. Yet she harbored no malice, entertained no fears. With each adjustment to reality, Lucy became increasingly more aware of God's presence within her. From this awareness came her strength. It was from this conviction that her actions sprang, that her sensitivity opened up, that her judgments unfolded.

Lucy also sensed the reality of her Teachers' sufferings, the rumors, the people's pessimism, the calumnies, the physical deprivations they had endured and were continuing to endure. Patiently her Teachers had arrested the fears of the poor who were alarmed at the possibility of the Schools' closing. Calmly they had assured the people that the School would not change its policy of providing for the material needs of their daughters.

The Teachers had worked indefatigably, going from house to house, encouraging and exhorting the girls to remain in School. They had continued to give the morning and evening meditations, very often on empty stomachs. How often they had shared their meager rations with the poor. Lucy thanked God for her Teachers and for their strength of character in the face of trial and tribulation. Her Teachers were growing as contemplatives-in-action. They were learning to find God in every situation; therefore they knew what it meant to pray always.

Lucy derived her greatest consolation from her Teachers' unity of spirit. No one shirked her responsibility; each Teacher contributed her best to create an atmosphere of joy and hope. Her Teachers, Lucy thought gratefully, were women in love, in love with Christ. They realized only too well that there could not be another Cardinal Barbarigo. No one would provide for them in the same manner he had. But they continued to trust that Divine Providence would never fail them. Courageously they continued their apostolate.

Utterly dependent on God yet rightfully independent among men, Lucy thrust herself into her work. She was responsible to and for her Teachers, her Schools, the poor, the sick, the dying, sinners. To them she owed her energy, her time, her love, and devotion. She had no time for self-pity, no room for fear.

The School at Grotte di Castro required immediate attention; it was one of the Cardinal's unfinished tasks. So, shortly after the funeral, Lucy traveled there to comfort and aid the struggling community. They were aware of their critical financial situation, but they also recognized Lucy's resourcefulness. Moreover, having her there with them restored their hope. They had no doubt that Lucy would find the means to restore the dilapidated School.

The earthquake had practically destroyed their building. The foundation needed strengthening; the roof had to be repaired; the walls had to be reinforced. Lucy estimated the cost; it was enormous. However, she had no choice but to make repairs. Closing the School was out of the question; the people needed the presence of the Teachers among them.

When Lucy explained the situation to her Teachers, the response was unanimous. They offered to cut down on expenses, determined to live even more simply. Their only concern, they declared, was to save the School. Lucy had to restrain their enthusiasm, but their zeal strengthened her. She left no stone unturned to solve their problems.

She sought out workers who were willing to wait for their pay. She searched out benefactors. She appealed to the commune for help. No one turned a deaf ear to her. Her determination aroused the admiration of the townspeople. As one they worked to restore their School. Her teachers remembered her frequently repeated maxim to them and were not surprised: "Be of good heart, do not fear; have confidence in God in all your troubles. God will provide for your needs in proportion to your faith." Lucy's confidence in God was without limit, and so was God's Providence.

In spite of the crowded hours there in Grotte, Lucy found time to give the morning and evening meditations to the women. She visited the sick, consoled the dying, contacted the alumnae. One afternoon she went to visit a poor woman who had accidentally hurt her arm. While trying to detach something from the wall, the unfortunate woman had caught her arm on a hooked nail. Gangrene had set in; amputation was mandatory. Lucy approached the suffering woman, made the sign of the cross on her arm and begged God to cure her *in the name of Cardinal Barbarigo.* Immediately the inflammation subsided; the wound closed. The operation was not necessary. (Often in the years ahead Lucy called upon the Cardinal for help. Never did he fail her.)

Promising to return very soon, Lucy bade farewell to the Teachers and townspeople of Grotte di Castro.

Lucy went next to Marta, the little fishing village, where conversion happened—slowly. Lucy usually prolonged her visit here. Her moral support was medicine to the long-suffering Teachers as well as to the faithful women and girls. Every day Lucy taught the adult classes and conducted spiritual exercises for the women. Every afternoon she visited the sick.

One day, during her stay in Marta, she went to see Egidia who had fallen from a horse and had broken a rib. The woman had been bedridden for six months, but there was no improvement. Lucy made the sign of the cross over Egidia and prayed to the Cardinal, begging him to intercede for Egidia. Again, *in the name of the Cardinal,* Lucy begged God to cure the stricken woman. Instantly Egidia was healed. Word of the miraculous cure spread rapidly; many more women came to the adult classes. Lucy sensed the Cardinal's presence as she spoke to the women about their responsibility as Christians; so did the women.

Lucy's visits always invigorated her community. Her intelligent observations and stimulating discussions challenged their minds. Her oneness with God ennobled them . . . inspired them. Her Teachers appreciated her presence among them; her departure always saddened them.

After Marta, Lucy stopped for a few days in each of the towns surrounding Lake Bolsena. Everywhere she investigated the orchards and farms, those already belonging to the Teachers and those she hoped to purchase or lease. Everywhere she checked the condition of the home-school, sought out benefactors who had voiced their intent to help. Everywhere she approached the authorities of the commune, urging them to lend their support to the Schools. Lucy had become a familiar figure everywhere. She was loved and respected by many. She was feared and disliked by some —those whose consciences she bothered.

Late in November, Lucy went to Tarquinia. She had already made several visits there since the epidemic early that year. The orphans and teachers were slowly recovering, but they needed so much more—more substantial food, warmer clothes, more domestic help.

As usual, her sister, Elizabeth, had outdone herself in generosity. She paid the salary for an extra cleaning woman and provided bread for the year. All through the year her gifts continued to arrive: fruit, candy, clothes. Elizabeth was Tarquinia's greatest benefactor.

Lucy never went to the orphanage empty-handed. Laden with fruit and candy, she greeted each orphan with a hug and a gift. The orphans loved their Teachers, but Lucy was their favorite. They were hers too.

While in Tarquinia, Lucy received word that the new bishop was to arrive late that December. Her place, therefore, was in Montefiascone. She wanted to greet him together with her Teachers at the motherhouse.

On the way home, Lucy reflected on the condition of the Schools. Materially speaking, there was much to be desired—her Teachers subsisted on so very little. Yet on the other hand, her Schools had taken root—deep root. The classes were crowded; in fact, the town streets were empty of children and young girls during the school day. The homes were feeling the impact of the girl-missionaries. Parishes were flourishing spiritually. Her Teachers, she thought fondly, were real women—selfless, generous, strong!

Then her thoughts rested on the new bishop. Lucy wondered about him. Having heard only good news about him, Lucy was hopeful.

Monsignor Sebastian Pompilio Bonaventuro was coming to the diocese of Montefiasonce-Tarquinia with a rich background in law, philosophy, and theology. He was also a noted educator, famous for the Seminary he had established in Gubbio. That Seminary, staffed by the most erudite professors in Europe, enjoyed universal applause.

Monsignor Bonaventuro, hand-picked by Pope Clement XI, came to his new diocese with special recommendations. The Holy Father had entrusted to him all the works begun by the Cardinal, but most particularly, the Pope had insisted that the bishop support and defend the Teaching Institute.

Monsignor Bonaventura was well-informed about his new pastorate; his brother, Monsignor Alessandro Bonaventura, was the Pope's almoner. From him the incoming bishop had learned the financial status of the diocese. From Monsignor Recchi he had heard about Lucy and the Schools and the Seminary. Monsignor Bonaventura was grateful for the financial concessions the Pope had made for the benefit of the Schools. He looked forward to continuing and improving the good works already begun by his predecessor.

Bishop Pompilio Bonaventura arrived in Montefiascone the last week of December 1706. He observed Lucy in action and approved. He noted particularly her prudence and dynamism in governing. Wisely the Bishop reconfirmed her as Directress of the Schools and Superior General of the Institute. Impressed by the good effects of the Schools, he solemnly promised to continue maintaining and supporting them at his own expense. Never did the Bishop fail in his promise. Every month he gave Lucy thirty *scudi* or more; it was the most he could afford. Although the Schools would not enjoy the financial ease of Barbarigo's time, they were at least guaranteed existence. They could function! For this Lucy was thankful.

Shortly after his arrival, Lucy called the Teachers to Montefiascone for a week-end. She wanted them to meet their new Bishop and to welcome him in their midst. It was on this occasion that he placed the Schools under the protection of the Blessed Virgin Mary under the title of Our Lady of the Presentation. He declared November 21 the Institute's special feast day.

It was also on this occasion that he announced the changes he had made in the teaching method. Everyone was stunned, including Lucy. The happiness she had tasted in his genuine concern and generosity turned bitter. It was like a desecration to the Cardinal's memory. Moreover, Lucy had experienced the wisdom and efficacy of the current method. She determined to point out its advantages to His Excellency. Perhaps he would retract his decision.

The method, as given by Rose Venerini and modified by Cardinal Barbarigo, was geared to serve the needs of the very poor. It was a simple method, marked by uncomplicated questions and answers, short spans of varied activities. Bishop Bonaventuro eliminated the simple questions and answers, retaining only the questions contained in the Bellarmine Catechism. He added long prayers to the daily program.

Lucy's respectful observations to the Bishop did not effect a change of mind. Having spoken her mind, Lucy obeyed. And she encouraged her Teachers to do the same. Again she reminded them that it was not the method which taught. *They* were the Teachers. The principles of the old method remained the same. It was their duty as Teachers to simplify the questions in the Bellarmine Catechism, to break up the long prayers with song and silent meditation. They had to adjust to each reality and discover in that reality new wisdom.

Bishop Bonaventuro was an innovator; he wanted to imprint his mark on the diocese. He suppressed the Teaching Branch of the Divine Love Congregation. He imposed on it strict papal enclosure. Of course, Catherine Comaschi and Don Morani rejoiced in this change. Lucy thanked God that she and her Teachers had not joined the group. Her intuitive wisdom had saved her Institute.

In the Seminary, the Bishop abolished the economic board. This was to prove disastrous for Lucy and the Schools.

Later that year, Lucy thought it wise to complete the settlement of the Cardinal's will. Many of the items willed to the Schools were housed in the Seminary. In all justice Lucy claimed the articles. But all she received was strong opposition. Under no circumstances would they relinquish the goods. Lucy was dumbfounded. To obtain what was legally hers, she had no choice but to resort to law. Moreover, her financial need was formidable.

Lucy detested the action she was forced to take. The Cardinal's charity had founded those institutions. He had dispossessed himself for them. Now here they were wasting money on lawsuits. Humbly she approached the authorities at the Seminary. Why couldn't they come together in peace and arbitrate as brothers and sisters? They agreed.

To that effect an act was drawn up for both parties by Lawrence Sanzonetti, Episcopal Chancellor and public notary. The aribtrator was Monsignor Bernard Recchi; he was well-informed. Having served as the late Cardinal's auditor and apostolic visitator for Clement XI, Monsignor Recchi knew the claims of both parties.

Monsignor Recchi decided that the Seminary actually owed the School four-hundred-seventy *scudi*. But in view of the fact that both parties had been dear to the Cardinal, he reduced the sum owed to four hundred *scudi,* if it were paid in a lump sum, or to ten *scudi* a year if paid in installments. If the Seminary refused to do this, however, Lucy would have every right to pursue the matter further. Neither party had the right to contradict the decision under any pretext. The act was promulgated on the 26th day of February, 1707.

Lucy accepted the verdict with quiet dignity. At first, so did the Seminary. But not for long! Disregarding Monsignor Recchi's decision, they reversed their stance and made new claims. Lucy maintained silence, as she had promised she would.

On November 10, 1707, for reasons never discovered by Lucy, Monsignor Recchi reduced the claims owed Lucy from 470 *scudi* to 20 scudi. This was a calamity for Lucy and the Schools. But Lucy continued in her silence. She would not offend the Cardinal's memory with further disputes. Her financial loss, balanced against the scandal of continued litigation, carried no weight.

Lucy received a large painting of St. Francis De Sales from the Seminary; that was all. She accepted it graciously. For Lucy, it was a closed issue.

Again Lucy proved herself a real woman—a radically Christian woman. She lived His word: "If anyone wants to go to law over your shirt, hand him your coat as well" (Matt. 5:40).

10

Expanding the Schools

*Would that I were many Lucys
so that multiplying myself I
could ceaselessly spread your
glory everywhere.*
—Lucy Filippini

THE YEAR 1707 registered an up and down scale of emotions for Lucy Filippini and her community. When, in the spring of that year, Clement XI summoned Lucy to Rome to open a school there, her song of love reached lyrical tones. Bishop Pompilio Bonaventura's enthusiastic response blended harmoniously with Lucy's eagerness "to be in every corner of the earth" so as to rhapsodize God's love to people everywhere. She yearned "to become many Lucys, so that multiplying herself, she could spread His glory everywhere."

Lucy could not contain her joy! She had to celebrate it with her dear friend, Rose Venerini. With her blessing, Lucy's elation would be complete.

A note of suffering blotted the rejoicing; Rose hesitated to bestow the desired blessing. Her reaction pained Lucy deeply. Although Lucy was aware that Rose disapproved the changes made in the method, she had not anticipated resistance.

The Ignatian didactic method, introduced into the Schools by Rose, had been replaced by the experiential, baroque-influenced approach. The Religious Teachers had imbibed the spirituality of their fathers and co-workers, the Pious Fathers, and the Schools reflected that spiritual evolution.

According to Rose Venerini, Lucy's Schools were no longer imparting a solid, rational education. According to Lucy and the Pious Fathers, the new approach to education was an effective blend of the academic with the spiritual. Lucy's Schools had converted from rational-objective places of learning to subjective Christian-academic laboratories. The revised curriculum, as well as the methodology, was geared to serve the needs of the poor who responded enthusiastically to the deductive method in an atmosphere which breathed the heart-filled piety of the day.

In both School systems, the students received an excellent Christ-centered education; only the *approach* to learning differed.

Father Martinelli, Rose's spiritual director, reasoned with Rose to change her mind with reminders that her young friend counted on her blessing. There was room in the world for a variety of approaches. Lucy, he reminded her, was a graced-Teacher; her spirit transcended every method.

As Rose listened, she envisioned Lucy's eager face, awaiting her approval. Finally, Rose's love for Lucy conquered her disapproval of the innovations. She agreed, furthermore, that Lucy did inspirit whatever method she used.

Rose's endorsement erased the blot her former refusal had imprinted. Lucy's joy was crowned.

The vigorous Institute rejoiced as one; their apostolic horizon was widening. One day they *would* be in "every corner of the earth." Lucy's Teachers wrote to her expressing their pride and joy. They promised to support her with their prayers. Their unity in the common vision underlined and punctuated every word. Their deep affection touched her; she felt humble in the bosom of so much love.

In the days before her departure for Rome, Lucy contemplated the brief history of the Institute. The Schools in Tarquinia and in the Lake Bolsena region were progressing slowly but definitely. Her Teachers were generating Christ in the hearts and minds of their students. The School at Grotte di Castro had been repaired and was functioning again. She blessed the loyalty and hard work of the people there. Lucretia Amari, the directress in Grotte, was an inspiration to the townspeople; Lucy thanked God for her gifts. The Teachers and orphans in Tarquinia were improving daily.

However many problems still remained: They were all very poor; there was too much instability of location; too many lacked gardens and orchards with which to support themselves.

The Schools in Montefiascone had suffered much . . . and it showed! The Teachers, especially those residing at the motherhouse, had experienced deep pain in the past three years. Most of those now assigned there had been either personally involved in the Monastery School or had been grieved because of it. They had borne the brunt of the gossip and slander without a murmur, without a word of self-justification. They had been powerless witnesses to the deterioration of the School.

One crisis had followed upon the other. Lucy had remained strong and serene. From her the Teachers were learning the deep meaning of faith-in-action. Nevertheless, the suffering had taken its toll on their physical health. Their constant exhaustion and struggles made the most sensitive among them easy victims to colds and to epidemics. Lucy was very much aware of their physical condition and spared no means to fortify both their bodies and their spirits. With loving care and active concern, she soothed their hurts and comforted them. Leaving them was the only reluctance Lucy experienced on the eve of her departure for Rome that May in 1707.

As Superior General of the Institute, it was Lucy's responsibility to open new foundations. Rome marked a definite turning point in the history of the community. For the very first time Lucy was opening a School *alone*—without Rose Venerini, without her Cardinal Barbarigo. For the very first time Lucy was opening a School outside the Montefiascone-Tarquinia Diocese.

The first Roman School was located on Chiave D'Oro, near Holy Spirit Monastery. Lucy had asked the Pious Fathers to help her find a suitable location. The Fathers, confident that St. Lawrence Parish would soon be under their jurisdiction, selected a house near the church.

It was a relief to learn that the Pope's Almoner, Monsignor

Alessandro Bonaventura, had been ordered to assume all expenses for the maintenance of the School. Lucy was free to work for and among the people without the burden of financial worries.

Also, for the first time Lucy was not opening a School in a rural area. Rome was a city in comparison to the rustic hamlets in Bolsena; Montefiascone and Tarquinia were villages by contrast. Rome was a fascinating city, saturated with the culture of the ages, a living history book. It was not only the seat of Christendom but also the ruling power in the Pontifical States. It was the home of renowned artists and philosophers, of adventurers, of ambitious politicians and clergymen, of tradesmen and farmers, of wealthy noblemen and destitute peasants. It was the home of many religious orders of men and women. It was the world in a city!

Rome was divided into sectors. Each one attracted its own class and formed an autonomous cultural entity. Each district had its own church around which its social activities revolved.

St. Lawrence Parish drew the poor together, the farmers and the struggling tradesmen. But they were Romans, and like all Romans, were a proud people. Their lifestyle, their manner of dress, their superiority complex pronounced loudly their sophisitication. The Roman woman was a sharp contrast to the country woman back home in Montefiascone.

The first time the Roman women saw Lucy, they were offended by her rough cloth dress; the women labeled her a simple peasant woman, nothing more. Out of curiosity, however, they accepted the pastor's invitation to hear Lucy explain her School program.

Her voice silenced their repugnance; it reflected a culture born of nobility. They found themselves listening intently to her message. Her words hit them like gentle pellets, vigorously, persuasively. She held them spellbound! She had power beyond the ordinary. Christ came alive through her words; they felt His pull. Suddenly their stilled spiritual emotions, long buried deep in superficialities, burst open. Lucy could not restrain their tears of remorse, of hope, and love. In Christ Lucy had once again conquered hearts *for Christ*.

The first school day caused a minor revolution in St. Lawrence Parish; homes emptied their female population to the School. Lucy needed assistance. She remembered the Cardinal's words: "Should classes be more numerous than Teachers, engage experienced, exemplary, and God-fearing women to help." Lucy did not have to look far; in fact, she did not have to look at all.

A young lady, Margaret Setoli, presented herself to Lucy and volunteered her services. Margaret came from a wealthy family, was well-educated, and deeply religious. She came highly recommended. Lucy accepted her on trial. It wasn't long before Margaret expressed her desire to join the Institute. Lucy, who knew how to read hearts, perceived her sincerity. She did not doubt Margaret's vocation.

As a postulant, Margaret received "on-the-job formation" with Lucy as her directress. It was a time of spiritual transfusion from Lucy to Margaret. From Lucy the young lady learned the contemplative-active nature of the Institute as well as the sacredness of her apostolate. She was a worthy disciple and learned quickly. Lucy recognized her talents and encouraged her to use them for God's glory.

With Margaret as her aid, Lucy was able to pursue the all-embracing activities she normally performed. The early morning and evening classes for women were crowded to over capacity; so was the class for the young girls whose ages ranged from seven to fourteen. Margaret stayed close to Lucy, observed her teach, imbibed her spirit, learned the method. Lucy afforded her many opportunities to grow as a Teacher, in the classroom and outside of it. Margaret's capable assistance was indispensable to Lucy.

The response to Lucy's teachings was impressive. The total neighborhood and its environs felt the impact of her enthusiasm. As in Montefiascone, Lucy's Roman School also went out into the streets to preach Christ's concern for all men. It traveled to the hospitals where Lucy and her most zealous students ministered to the sick. They fed the helpless, bathed them, cut their nails, combed their hair, changed their bedding. In short, they restored their dignity. Their ministrations healed more than the physical. Patiently the girls, the women, Lucy, and Margaret taught the patients simple prayers, reviewed the truths of the faith, soothed their inner pains, and inspired them to offer their sufferings to God for the conversion of sinners. Life took on new meaning for the abandoned sick in those ill-fated hospitals.

Young girls and older women began to shed their superficialities as their understanding of Christian womanhood deepened. Husbands, fathers and fiancés recognized the changes in their women and reacted accordingly. Modesty became the trademark of Lucy's students; a gentle, active concern for their neighbor their distinguishing feature. Their spirit of mortification edified; the intensity of their prayer-life inspired.

Lucy's Roman School-without-walls was reaching down to the very roots of society dramatically.

It was in Rome that Lucy, for the first time, was spontaneously called *Holy Teacher* by the common people. Disregarding Lucy's rough garb, the Romans had discovered the "saint."

One of Lucy's first Roman students, who later became a Religious Teacher, often recounted how she also had been repelled by Lucy's dress. She had attended the School, she declared, only because her parents had insisted. In one day, however, Lucy had won her over completely. Lucy's sweet manner and vivacious teaching made school a paradise. The young lady found every excuse to stay after school just to be near Lucy. It was a special privilege to spend the night at the convent. Lucy had magnetic power over the girls! To please God alone became the absorbing ambition of her students, young and old.

In the Montefiascone-Tarquinia Diocese, the spiritual exercises for the rich and the poor were one and the same. Lucy, recognizing the psychological needs of the lower class in her home-diocese, had invited the rich to attend the exercises. The presence of the nobility at the spiritual exercises gave the poor a certain sense of importance and prestige.

In Rome, however, the common people did not require the company of the aristocracy to draw them to the spiritual exercises. Class distinctions in Rome were marked. To be a Roman satisfied the need for prestige no matter what the social standing happened to be. So in Rome Lucy held separate spiritual exercises for the aristocracy.

Princess Altieri Borromea, a woman of great piety, was among the first who attended the exercises for the nobility. The Princess immediately recognized Lucy's deep spirituality; each one saluted the mature Christ in the other! A beautiful and undying friendship was born. In later years, whenever Lucy visited Rome, the Princess always invited Lucy to her home. During Lucy's absence from Rome, an exchange of letters resembling shared prayer dialogues sustained the relationship. Their friendship, rooted in Christ, grew with every encounter. The Princess became an invaluable ally in the difficult days awaiting Lucy. She was one of the Institute's greatest benefactors.

In Rome the spiritual exercises followed the usual format. The women gathered in the room set aside for them. The windows were closed and the blinds drawn to shut out the noise and distractions of the streets. After a prayer service, Lucy preached as only a woman immersed in Christ could. Her words pierced their hearts.

An interval of silence followed her message. During this space of time, the women meditated on the spoken words. The silence provided the women the opportunity to examine their lives in the light of the message Lucy had given. Often the response was exuberant. Unrestrained, remorseful sobs mingled with and often overpowered the clamor in the streets. Passersby heard the cries and questioned the cause of the emotional outbursts.

Very often public sinners attended the sessions. Some came on a dare; others came to find peace. Still others came at Lucy's express invitation. Lucy gently uncovered the camouflaged fears of the would-be scorners. She helped the peace-seekers find tranquility through self-acceptance and trust in God. Every conversion was a spiritual drama in action.

Lucy had great compassion for wayward women. She sought them out wherever they were. Some of the ladies in her morning and evening classes informed her that a house of prostitution was located on Euphemia Street. Many of her students passed that house every day on the way to school; this fact disturbed her. But even more disturbing was the thought of those poor, lost women who desperately sought happiness in self-destruction. Lucy could not rest until she acted upon the word spoken to her by the concerned ladies in her class. Her zeal for God's honor and her boundless charity for sinners filled her with courage and authority.

Her head held high, her eyes ablaze with love, Lucy dared to enter that house. Gently she spoke to the women, assuring them of God's undying love for them. Her compassionate manner removed the sting from the reproaches she made. Her selfless love for them broke down the barriers they built against a grasping world. Many did abandon their way of life. When they had no home to return to, or if they were too embarrassed to go back, Lucy gave them lodging in a room below the School. She was not unaware of the criticism her action precipitated, but her overriding concern for sinners blocked out self-concern and fear.

When Lucy harbored the repentant women, tongues wagged and calumniated. Lucy pitied those who were scandalized. Yet she could not allow their bigotry to determine her response to God's call to spread His Kingdom. "Even if all the men of the world with all the demons of hell persecute me and desire my ruin, I firmly hope that God will never abandon me."

Undaunted, Lucy continued her work of love! She could not and would not abandon the repentent sinners. She had to help them walk with the Lord again. Their bodies, as well as their self-dignity, needed to be restored. They had to find respectable work.

So Lucy fed them, housed them, taught them, found jobs for them. She befriended them to the end. Even after they found stability, Lucy maintained her contact with them. Roman cynics kept careful notes.

Lucy never wavered in her mission to restore women to God. Notified that an orgy was in the offing, Lucy hurried to the designated location and advanced fearlessly into the room where the licentious festivities were about to take place. With her right index finger pointed at the men and the left finger at the door, she pronounced one word only—"Out." Under the fire of her piercing eyes, "out" they did go. An infuriated Lucy had frightened the men away. They had been powerless against the strength of her zeal. But a transformed Lucy fixed her eyes on the frustrated women. A merciful, gracious Lucy confronted the rebellious women. Fearlessly Lucy spoke to them. Gradually her soft voice, warm with compassion, calmed the tempest within them. Never, however, were these battles against sin easy victories. But always Lucy stood her ground. Her words were gently strong, softly piercing. Her whole being, one with Christ, embraced them and urged them to repent. Some did return home, healed. Lucy always invited them to attend the spiritual exercises. Only God's grace could provide the strength they needed not to return to their fallen way of life.

Suspicious Romans marked down her every move. They began to spread rumors about Lucy, saying she was both a follower and teacher of Quietistic doctrines. A few ecclesiastics picked up these rumors and brought them to the Holy Office, denouncing her for teaching the doctrines of Michael Molinos.

Romans, and especially Roman ecclesiastics, had long memories. Though the founder of Quietism in Rome had died ten years before Lucy's arrival in the eternal city, the members of the Sacred Inquisition would not allow themselves to forget those tragic days. Nor could they; neo-followers kept cropping up when least expected. So their search for possible offenders was constant.

Reverend Michael Molinos, a native of Spain who entered Rome in 1663, had no difficulty spreading his Quietistic theology. Quietism blended very well with the tenets of a hedonistic society and political opportunists.

Molinos taught that union with God is achieved by abandoning all thoughts of oneself and by achieving complete passivity. In this state, Molinos insisted, one becomes absorbed in the contemplation of God and divine things. Thus he becomes a perfect instrument of God's will.

Quietism is a form of mystical theology in which spiritual contact with God goes beyond reason and emotion. According to the Quietists, one should not actively use any of the powers of his soul. Perfection, they claimed, could be achieved only by contemplation and absolute passivity. Molinos placed so much emphasis on passivity in prayer that his followers rejected the efficacy of the sacraments, the necessity of good works or of works of penance, and the use of devotional practices.

Molinos exhorted his penitents not to struggle against evil inclinations. He went so far as to claim that all personal effort was evil because God wished to work in the individual soul without its cooperation. The soul, he taught, was to remain passive when besieged by temptation, neither consenting nor resisting. Thus did one attain the self-annihilation which leads to union with God. Having achieved this quiet state of contemplation, one could not commit sin.

Quietism, followed to its logical conclusion, had, of course, dangerous consequences. *In the name of God,* Molinos and his followers committed lurid brutalities and lived dissolute lives. Yet outwardly he and his followers appeared as pious people, "intent on doing God's will."

Michael Molinos preached perfect abandonment to God through contemplation. Having renounced the use of his free will, he claimed he could no longer sin. So from 1675–1687 he continued to offer the Sacrifice of the Mass without ever going to confession. When he was faced with the temptation to commit fornication, he did not resist, but rather he became a "passive accomplice to God's will."

So, when Lucy Filippini gathered women together and led them in mental prayer . . . when Lucy harbored wayward women in the School . . . when Lucy sought spiritual direction from the Pious Fathers, one of whom had been unjustly denounced a Quietist, the conclusion drawn by superficial observers and righteous bigots seemed appropriate. They concluded that Lucy was a follower of Molinos, a Quietist; that she was a hypocrite who preached contemplation and love of God while harboring bad women in her School.

Among her accusors were shallow-brained ecclesiastics who could not distinguish between what was true and what was false piety. There were also calloused inquisitors who refused to admit that Lucy preached not only contemplation but also good works, mortification, and moral responsibility for one's actions; that Lucy encouraged her followers to make retribution for their sins, to receive the sacraments frequently, to increase their devotional practices; that Lucy's loving concern for wayward women was purely God-centered; and that Lucy desired heaven and feared hell. Lucy's friends trembled for her. They begged her to be careful, to be more cautious.

But Lucy did not lose her serenity; her conscience was clear. Her theology was in keeping with the teachings of the Church. If the clergy wished to sit in when she preached to the women, they were welcome. She had nothing to fear. That they questioned the repentant sinners living in the School did not surprise her. Did not the people also criticize Christ when He dined with sinners? Lucy regretted the shortsightedness of men who judged actions on mere appearances.

However, at the precise moment when definite action was about to be taken against her, Divine Providence intervened. Lucy received an emergency communication from Bishop Bonaventura recalling her to Montefiascone. An epidemic had struck the Montefiascone area; her Teachers were ill and had no one to care for them. Those who were not sick were discouraged and depressed. A few Schools had been discontinued for the interim. It was the first week of December, 1707; Lucy had been in Rome seven months.

During these seven months, Lucy had run the School, taught, performed her social apostolate and had given spiritual direction to Margaret Setoli, whom she had accepted as candidate to her Teaching-Community. Though Lucy had no doubt whatsoever concerning Margaret's vocation, she realized she could not leave her alone to administer the School in Rome. Margaret was still too young and inexperienced. On the other hand, Lucy had no substitute Teacher in Montefiascone whom she could summon to Rome. Yet Lucy knew she had no choice but to return home; her sick Teachers needed her. Lucy had but one alternative: to call upon Rose Venerini. Determined to settle the matter as quickly as possible, Lucy wrote to Rose explaining the problem. If Rose could replace her for the duration of the epidemic, then Lucy could return to Montefiascone, her mind at ease. Lucy also informed Rose that Margaret Setoli, whom she would invest before leaving for Montefiascone, would remain in Rome to help her. She assured

Rose that Margaret would be invaluable to her. She ended by begging Rose not to delay her arrival.

Rose did not postpone her arrival. When the students saw Rose in the school building, they feared the worst. Their Lucy was going to leave them! It was impossible for Lucy to hide the truth from them. The students were inconsolable; they pleaded with her not to go away. The emergency which had called her home held no meaning for them. Lucy assured them that Rose was an excellent teacher, that they would learn to love her. Nothing Lucy said could quench their tears. Therefore, Lucy decided that her departure had to be at an early hour, before the arrival of the students.

Lucy not only admired her old friend's capability as a teacher, but, more importantly, revered her as a holy woman. Rose, she felt sure, would soon dispel her students' grief.

The following day the classroom resembled a wake! Rose tried every means to cheer the sobbing girls. It was impossible! Their hearts and minds were with Lucy. No one, they insisted, could replace her.

Several days later the girls, exhausted with sorrow, appeared ready to be taught again. Rose began to teach them but according to her own method. Lucy's method was foreign to her character and contrary to her principles. The girls could not adjust to Rose's ways and manner of teaching. Whereas Lucy had allowed them the freedom to perform exercises of piety according to their particular dispositions, Rose forbade them to do so. Whereas Lucy began with the known and gradually led them to discover the unknown, Rose expected them to begin with the unknown. The formal classroom atmosphere Rose created depressed the girls; their interest in school waned. First a few, then more and more began to absent themselves. Within the month, the number of girls attending school dropped drastically.

The Pious Fathers witnessed the daily withdrawal and were indignant; they knew the reason for the failure. The Pontifical Almoner, who, during a former visit to the School, had rejoiced in its obvious success now found the contrast tragic. He was extremely disturbed.

Rose Venerini was distraught. Rose, a sedate, religious woman trained by the Jesuit Fathers, was incapable of adopting Lucy's method; it was against her nature. The girls needed time to adjust, she thought. Rose sincerely believed her way better, more efficacious. If only they would give her a chance, she knew she could prove it.

The criticism voiced by the Pious Fathers irritated Rose. The displeasure expressed by the Pontifical almoner humiliated her. In her constant correspondence with Father Martinelli, Rose cried out her anguish. Father Martinelli urged her to persevere. Eventually, he consoled her, she would prove the advantages of her method in one of her own Schools in Rome. He reminded her that her presence in Rome was a providential breakthrough. It afforded her the opportunity to make herself and her School System known to the Romans. However, he continued, if she found it impossible to make a dent in the present mentality, then she should ask permission to leave. Her Schools in Viterbo continued to need her.

Rose had been in Rome less than four months when she departed for Viterbo.

Margaret Setoli was alone in a school emptied of students. The Pontifical Almoner, at the instigation of the Pious Fathers, took immediate action. Monsignor Bonaventura wrote to his brother, the Bishop of Montefiascone, informing him of the disastrous situation. He petitioned him either to send Lucy back or to assign one of her Teachers to Rome to restore the School according to Lucy's method. The urgency of the communication moved the Bishop to respond promptly.

The epidemic was over; the Teachers were doing well; the Schools in Montefiascone had reopened and were slowly but surely progressing. Lucy suggested that the Bishop send two of her best Teachers to Rome; she could spare them now, she assured him.

The bells of St. Lawrence pealed the welcome news: the Teachers from Montefiascone were coming to Rome to work among them.

Imbued with the spirit of their foundress, marked by docility and gentility, Lucy's Teachers also attracted followers. How often they had heard Lucy exclaim, "My daughters, the human spirit is such that it abhors rigor. Severity loses all, breaks hearts, generates hate. If it does good, it does so with bad grace; no one appreciates it." With a deep understanding of the particular needs of the poor entrusted to their care, Lucy's Teachers taught according to the method handed down to them by Lucy and the Cardinal. Again the School went out to the farms, to the homes. Young girls and women listened and heard the sincere concern of the Teachers who knew how to touch the hearts of simple people whose cultural horizons were limited.

And, once again the streets of St. Lawrence Parish were emptied of girls during school hours. The School continued to grow until the walls could hold no more.

11

Threatening Times

I implore you, I beseech you,
that none of these whom we
find gathered in this place be
lost. May all of them praise you
for all eternity
—Lucy Filippini

CLEMENT XI, SHORTLY after his election in 1700, formally approved the French Philip of Anjou as rightful heir to the Spanish throne. As a result of this action, a short war erupted between the papal states and Emperor Joseph I. When in 1709 the Austrians invaded the papal states and threatened to sack Rome, Clement XI was forced to favor the cause of the Austrian Hapsburg. But not until the Treaty of Utrecht in 1713, which finally recognized Philip of Anjou as Philip V of Spain, did the War of Spanish Succession come to an end.

During these years, imperial forces from Spain and from Naples stationed themselves throughout the Italian peninsula, including the territory of the papal states. To maintain the armies, heavy taxes were placed on the people, and farmers were forced to contribute food for the sustenance of the soldiers.

In addition to the miseries caused by war, there followed earthquakes, floods, famine, and a series of flu and malaria epidemics. The Montefiascone-Tarquinia diocese was one of the most hard-hit areas.

Only a faith-filled woman like Lucy Filippini could find within herself the strength, the courage, and the perseverance to overcome the overwhelming obstacles she met every step of the way. During these trying times, Lucy was constrained to assume many roles. She became the ingenious provider, the compassionate nurse, the astute businesswoman, the prudent conciliator. Everywhere she went she labored to reawaken, to regenerate, to reconcile her valiant but struggling Teaching-Community and her suffering people.

Grotte di Castro had once again been partially destroyed by an earthquake. In Montefiascone the restoration of the School was a steep, uphill process. In Tarquinia malaria continued to inflict suffering and death. Everywhere living conditions were deplorable; people were discouraged. The Schools were on the decline.

Though Bishop Bonaventura appreciated all that Lucy and her Teachers were doing in his diocese, a subtle difference separated the provident care he generously bestowed from the plenitude Cardinal Barbarigo had lavished on the Teachers. Bishop Bonaventura had not fathered the inspiration, had not suffered through the birth pangs of the incarnated idea. The good Bishop had not tasted the thrill of the infant Schools' first faltering steps. The Bishop's providence naturally lacked the founder's spark; it lacked the fastidiousness of a father who anticipates eleventh hour needs. A more salient reason, however, also contributed to the difference—Bishop Bonaventura's meager personal wealth. He could not afford the "extras" required to keep the girls in school, at least not to the extent the Cardinal had provided.

Lucy's Religious Teachers, imbued with the spirit of mortification, braved the reality of their predicament without complaint. After all, were they not graduates from Lucy Filippini's School of the Cross? There they had learned that only Divine Providence supplies ultimate peace and security. There they had learned that in "their hearts should reign one ambition, to desire and seek nothing more ardently and earnestly than the Kingdom of God and His justice. Then, when they least expected it, God Himself would tenderly and generously provide for them." There, in Lucy's School of Formation, they had learned to need nothing, to share all. "The Teachers should exercise due restraint in providing for their own needs, but for the needs of their neighbors they should be liberal and generous . . . ."

This crisis-filled time strengthened their faith in God and

renewed their dedication to spread the Kingdom of Christ. In an effort to keep the Schools open, to make it possible for the older girls especially to continue attending school, the Teachers deprived themselves of everything but the bare necessities. They economized, ate frugal meals, stretched their minimal allowance to the vanishing point. To bring in added revenue, they sold their needlework to the wealthy. Everything they received, either as salary or as gift, they shared generously—to the advantage of their students. Nonetheless, their hard-earned providence, generously distributed, failed to recoup the valid needs of the poverty-stricken families. Parents were often constrained by sheer necessity to send their older girls to the fields.

Undaunted, the Teachers brought the School to the fields. During the workers' rest periods, they taught them the basics of good Christian living. During the working hours, the Teachers led the girls in song and prayer; often they joined them in their labor. All this the Teachers did after a full day in school with the very young who continued to attend classes. But what was most beautiful was the joy with which they did everything.

Every night the Teachers drained by their ministry, fell on their knees—exhausted in body but invigorated in spirit. From the integrity of the interior life, the dynamism of their apostolate overflowed and promoted the Kingdom of heaven.

Lucy was very much aware of the tremendous sacrifices her Teachers were making for the sake of the apostolate. She was edified by her Teachers' docile response to the needs of the poor. However, their total selflessness did not surprise her; she had witnessed it countless times. In fact, it was this complete disregard for self-comfort which tugged at her heartstrings and compelled her to take action immediately.

Lucy, the contemplative-in-action, viewed the world with the eyes of her Lord and master; she listened and heard His Word within herself, within others, and within every circumstance. Lucy lived in His Presence constantly, twenty-four hours a day. During the day, she acted upon the Word she heard. During the night, she slept the sleep of ecstatic contemplation in the Divine embrace of

Her Crucified Lord. Spiritual slumber had long supplanted her need for normal sleep. Often the Teachers, who slept in adjacent rooms, heard her sing songs of rapture and adoration during the night. Her music, however, did not disturb their rest; instead it provided a refreshing background for those who were daily witnesses to her sanctity.

Lucy greeted each new day with zest, alive to the urgencies of each moment. After having spent the early morning hours in prayer before the Blessed Sacrament, Lucy plunged into her day's work, keenly conscious of the spiritual and material state of her Institute.

With the Cardinal gone, Lucy now had to assume the responsibility of securing stability for the Schools, of soliciting benefactors, of establishing trust funds, of obtaining endowments. She had to safeguard the health of her Teachers, first of all, by relieving some of the tensions; and secondly, by providing and insisting upon reasonable leisure time for them.

As soon as the Teachers in Montefiascone were well enough to take care of themselves, Lucy set about to accomplish her objectives.

In Gradoli, Grotte, Valentano and Latera, Lucy found benefactors whose funds she used to enlarge the Home-Schools belonging to the Institute, to replace rented locations with permanent Home-Schools, to purchase orchards and garden lots wherever needed. In Latera, Don Domenic Canepuccia, the Pastor, went a step further—he endowed the School.

In the three years from 1708 to 1711, this active-contemplative woman bought sixty-three properties. Some she purchased with the little money she inherited from the Cardinal; some with donations received from benefactors; but most were bought with the funds provided by the Cardinal's nephew, Monsignor Francis Mary Barbarigo, and by Lucy's sister, Elizabeth.

By 1712 every School in the Montefiascone-Corneto diocese enjoyed permanent stability of location. Every Home-School had a garden and an orchard. Every School had sufficient funds at its disposal to distribute hemp for the girls' dowries and bread for the poor. To insure future financial security, Lucy thought it wise to concentrate all stable goods and funds at the motherhouse in Montefiascone. Thus it was possible for all the Schools in the diocese to benefit from the common fund and the consolidated goods according to their particular needs.

Business transactions did not occupy all of Lucy's daytime; in fact they did not occupy even most of her time. Her industrious efforts were ingrained into the larger context of her primary goal, the building of God's Kingdom on earth.

Lucy solicited aid from benefactors, repaired buildings, bought properties, invested funds *during, between,* and *after* her customary activities. She continued to supervise her Schools, visiting each of them twice a year. She gave the morning and evening meditations, conducted the spiritual exercises, directed postulants, and never neglected the thousand and one duties which were hers as Superior General.

For Lucy, insuring the stability and future security of the Schools was a sacred mission. In her appeal to potential benefactors, Lucy stressed the dignity of their role, calling them co-missionaries. She assured them that their gift, graced by divine love, was not philanthropy, but charity. They were indispensable promoters of God's work on earth. Lucy's words pierced their logic and placed riches in their true perspective. In the clear light of Lucy's sincerity, benefactors felt enriched for having given.

To her Teachers, Lucy recommended, "Once the support of the Schools has been established so that they can sufficiently maintain themselves and even help the needy Schools in the same diocese, the Teachers *should not* be solicitious to seek additional wealth. They should be prudent and cautious about accepting legacies and bequests since they should not be concerned with accumulating wealth, but with saving souls."

From 1711 to 1730, Lucy founded nine other Schools in Rome and many others in the little towns of Upper Lazio—in Acquasparta, Acquapendente, Bagnorea; in Tuscany at the invitation and under the protection of Duke Cosino III of the Medici (Pitigliano, Montemarano, Onano); in Tolfa, Nepi, Aspia, Viano, under the protection of the House of Altieri; and in Scansano and

Rocca di Papa. By 1730 Lucy had opened approximately fifty-two Schools.

Before opening the School in Acquasparta, Lucy conducted the spiritual exercises for the women of the parish. The spiritual benefits of the retreat were, as usual, dramatic. But Lucy's success with the women brought her under public scrutiny. Again the ugly rumor that Lucy was a follower of Molinos raised its head. Clergymen were suspicious of her mental prayer sessions. Bigots were scandalized at the novelty of a woman-preacher and questioned her interest in public sinners. Skeptics doubted her piety and called it hypocrisy. News of the suspicion reached the spiritual leader of the diocese, Cardinal Gualterio.

Though previously the Cardinal had not entertained any doubts about Lucy, he now felt impelled to take precautionary measures. He ordered an investigation of Lucy's method of prayer as well as of the pious practices used during the exercises. He further commanded that the commissaries of the Holy Office living in Todi examine Lucy rigorously. So they did! They attended every lecture, examined her doctrine, experienced her prayer-workshops. Lucy passed every test; everything was absolutely orthodox. Moreover, the men were edified by her peace and composure despite the criticism. The commissaries gave her full license to continue her good work.

To be mistrusted by the very Church she loved was for Lucy the unspeakable anguish.

Lucy's charity towards her persecutors as well as her serenity during the bitter trial made a deep impression on the women of Acquasparta. In fact, their enthusiasm and zeal to follow Christ grew as they watched her suffering so patiently. When Lucy expressed her desire to found a School among them, the women were overjoyed. Two young experienced teachers approached Lucy at the end of the week and asked to be admitted into her Teaching Community.

Lucy's extraordinary intuitive gift enabled her to recognize them as worthy candidates. They were exemplary young women whose lifestyle had already prepared them for community living. Without hesitation, Lucy not only shortened the period of formation but also went a step further. At the end of a very brief novitiate, Lucy commissioned them to open the School in Acquasparta. The date was April 15, 1711.

In Scansano, the stigma of Quietism followed her. The Holy Office in Rome asked for information about her from the Vicar of that town. The following report reached Rome:

July 6, 1719

Two foreign women arrived in Scansano the evening of May 14. For eight days they remained in Mr. Tenente Pippi's empty house; the gentleman volunteered the use of his home to them; he stayed with Mr. Proposto for the eight days. After the spiritual exercises, they all returned to Montermarano.

One of the women was Signora Lucia, the other Signora Santa. Lucia is about thirty-five years old.* She is directress of the conservatory in Montefiascone, a native of Corneto. Santa is about twenty-six or twenty-seven years old, and is directress of the School in Pitigliano. During their eight-day stay, they gave daily spiritual exercises, two times a day. Each session lasted four hours.

The Exercises consisted of one and one-half hours of spiritual reading followed by meditation or mental prayer. The home was filled to capacity, with women, priests, and men (the latter were in adjoining rooms).

I attended every day. On the last day, Santa sang the Lauds; she has a beautiful voice.

They had permission from the Bishop to conduct these exercises. They had done the same in Montemarano.

Lucy is back in Montefiascone now. She has many young people under her direction.

There were no disorders during the exercises, except that some women fainted from the heat and lack of ventilation.

(Signed) Nicolo Ranieri
Vicar of Holy Office of Scansano

The Holy Office sent this letter to Bishop Bonaventura on July 22, 1719. Bishop Bonaventura wrote a response immediately. He praised Cardinal Barbarigo's work, expressed his esteem for the Schools and for the Teachers in the following words:

---

*Lucy was actually forty-seven at the time.

All the Teachers are unmarried women noted for their virtues and exemplary lives. Before they are commissioned to the Schools, they come to Montefiascone for several months or years of instruction, according to the need of each person. Lucy Filippini is their directress; she is a spirited maiden, certainly not an ordinary woman. She is the Superior General and Directress of all her Schools. She is sought out by many Bishops to open Schools in their dioceses. Lucy does everything with permission.

After giving a brief history of the Institute, the Bishop spoke his praise and esteem for the Institute and voiced quiet anger at the uncalled-for suspicion.

Never again did Lucy have to explain her actions to the church publicly.

Lucy Filippini was a contemporary of Leonard of Port Maurice, one of the greatest preachers of his day. Very often Lucy conducted retreats for women in the very same towns where Leonard had recently preached or where he would be going in the near future. Without being told, Leonard always knew when Lucy had preceded him. Lucy left her indelible mark on the women whose lives she touched. They prayed more devoutly, received the sacraments more often and dressed more modestly than other women. Whenever Lucy followed Leonard, very often she was able to accomplish what her friend had not succeeded in achieving, especially among the women.

In Montemarano Lucy preached a retreat several weeks after Leonard of Port Maurice had given a mission. Though many conversions had taken place at the time of the mission, there still remained several hardened prostitutes and obstinate men whom Leonard had not been able to reach.

Proud that one of their sex was the preacher, the good women of Montemarano flocked to the church in great numbers. But the prostitutes came also, not to hear the word of God but to ridicule it. Unscrupulous men who had rejected Leonard also went to hear her; they also intended to treat God's Word with derision. Since the exercises were for women only, the men climbed the roof, removed several pieces of thatches, and listened.

The crucifixion and death of Jesus Christ was Lucy's great

passion. It was always the subject of one of her talks. It was the message the men on the roof heard that day.

Lucy's deep involvement with the mystery never failed to carry her into ecstasy. Her face, illumined by grace, spoke her eloquent message; love-seared words sparkled forth from somewhere deep within her. They scorched the hearts of her listeners. Tearfully, they heard her closing remarks:

> I would accept even the cross and be crucified for Jesus Christ as He willingly did for me. I would not hesitate to give my life, not once but a thousand times, so that all men would be converted. May Jesus make us all burn with His Divine Life. I beg you, dear Lord, that as many as are here today, not one is lost, but rather that all of us praise You for all eternity.

The tough-skinned men on the roof had listened idly at first; they had been waiting for the right moment to hurl ridicule. It was never to be! Lucy's words had hit them hard. Jumping down from the roof, they rushed to the priest; they wanted to make their peace with God. One of the men later became a hermit.

In Veroli, the women moved to tears, cried out, "This woman has stolen our hearts; we would refrain from eating or sleeping only to hear her and stay with her."

In Onano Lucy was greeted with insults and stones. At her departure eight days later, the women, fervent in their remorse, accompanied her out to the gate of the town. They begged her to return soon.

Extreme vanity prevailed in Pitigliano. On the first day of the exercises, the women came dressed as if for a ball, in the latest baroque fashions, adorned with flowers, ribbons, and jewels. Lucy made no comment. But by the eighth day, modesty became the permanent way of life for the women. Lucy's sweet manner had conquered their hearts and their wills. Of their own accord, the women despoiled themselves of their vain dress.

One day, in Pitigliano, Lucy's ardor drew Christ to her miraculously. Lucy had gone to Pitigliano to supervise the School. Early one morning she and another Teacher left the town to attend Mass in the small church of St. Francis, a half-kilometer away. After a long wait, the priest entered the sanctuary, then proceeded to a side altar where the Blessed Sacrament was not reserved. Whenever Mass was offered at a side altar, Holy Communion was not distributed to the people.

Lucy, her heart splintered by longing for her sacramental Lord, moaned. Every fiber of her being yearned for Him! Every drop of her lifeblood cried, "Come, Jesus, come." Over and over, with every breath, she cried out. Weightless with desire, Lucy reached and touched the very heart of God. Her heart became His living chalice.

The broken particle of the host escaped the priest's chalice and flew to Lucy. Lucy's companion witnessed the miracle and was transfixed. The priest suffered consternation.

Several hours later, Lucy was still ecstatic in the Divine Embrace of her Beloved. Not so the confused priest, whose search for the missing particle was fruitless. Lucy's companion understood the good man's dilemma. To put his mind at ease she confided the happening to him. On their way home Lucy simply praised God; in His mercy God had heard her yearning cry to receive Him in Holy Communion and had fulfilled her desire. Her "soul magnified the Lord."

Pitigliano was a town in Tuscany ruled by Cosimo III. During his lifetime the Schools in Tuscany suffered no want. All benefactions ceased, however, with the death of Cosimo III in 1723; thereafter the Teachers had to live on what they earned and on what the charity of their people provided.

Nicolo Ciacci, Vicar General of Tuscany, wrote to Lucy stating he thought it imprudent and presumptuous to have more than one Teacher in Pitigliano. He could not afford the luxury of two.

Lucy answered by return mail. Sternly she reproved his lack of faith in Divine Providence and his lack of understanding of the need for human companionship.

Ciacci's response was a smiling acceptance of the reproval. Her faith, he said, more than made up for his deficiency. Gladly he would accept two, three, or four Teachers, as many as she could spare. He would love and appreciate them equally. He trusted God would reward her faith, not his lack of it. And God did, over and above Ciacci's most exaggerated dreams.

United as one in their appreciation for the Teachers, the common people pledged themselves to support the School no matter what it would cost them. Benefactors, previously reluctant to donate monies, generously endowed the School.

During these productive years, Lucy was a pilgrim, traveling from Rome to Montefiascone to Tuscany and back. In 1711, her School in Rome, St. Lawrence, having outgrown its walls, was transferred to another location and became St. Agatha of the Mountains. That same year, Lucy founded four more Schools in Rome; by 1725, six more.

St. Agatha became the central meeting place for the Roman Schools. Every Friday, the Teachers gathered there for the weekend—to share larger community experiences, to rest, to nourish the spirit which made them one.

The Teachers in the Bolsena area also gathered together once a week—sometimes in a secluded field where they celebrated community in prayer and song and picnic, sometimes in one of the larger Schools.

Lucy divided her time among the gathered communities spread throughout central and upper Italy. On these occasions, Lucy provided on-going formation sessions for her Teachers. Always she reminded them of their obligation to live prophetic lives. Lucy stressed docility to God's will, emphasized the need to pray always, encouraged them to work hard and to be self-supporting. To bear fruit, she said, the Teacher must die to self. Lucy recommended interior mortification over exterior but expressed the need for both. Her words fell on ground made fertile by her example.

Lucy also used these occasions to solicit her Teachers' views concerning decisions she was called to make. In her humility, Lucy never considered her lone opinion sufficient. The decisions finally taken by Lucy bore the marks of a harmonious community, united in spirit and purpose.

Their unanimity attracted attention! In every town the Schools had ardent followers as well as vehement antagonists. Appreciative men blessed the Teachers for the goodness restored to their homes.

Frustrated men cursed them for reawakening consciences. The selfless clergymen delighted in the praises extended to the Teachers. The self-centered churchmen bristled over the honor given the Teachers and for the influence exerted by them. The redeemed women celebrated their womanhood in Christ. The obstinate ones ridiculed the invitation to celebrate. So it was that the years between 1708 and 1720 formed a mosaic of triumphs and trials, of lights and shadows.

12

Accused, Defamed, Condemned

> *Even though all men should
> leave me and I were abandoned
> and forsaken by all my friends
> and relatives, I have strong hope
> that my God will never leave me
> because He will still be my
> Father.*
> —Lucy Filippini

DARKENING SHADOWS overcast the flood of light energized by Lucy Filippini's Schools.

In Gradoli, Canon Cocchi, an unscrupulous opportunist, played on Bishop Bonaventura's solicitude for the Teachers in an effort to gain his own end. Canon Cocchi coveted the Teachers' home. His plan to possess it revolved around a clause in the deed of purchase, fixed therein by Cardinal Barbarigo. It stated that, should the Teachers leave the School, the house should then become the property of the Collegiate Church.

In 1723, an epidemic struck Gradoli; among its victims were the Teachers. Canon Cocchi pounced upon the attendant conditions. He forwarded to Bishop Bonaventura a concerned-saturated communication informing him of the Teachers' poor health. He suggested that the Bishop order them home to Montefiascone. There, relieved of all tensions, they could rest. The urgency of the message threw dust into the Bishop's eyes and made him an innocent accomplice. He ordered the Teachers home.

Lucy hurried to the scene, aware that the Canon's "consideration" masked a cunning scheme. Father Polidori, the

Teachers' confessor, confirmed Lucy's suspicions. He promised to intercede for them with the Bishop. Fearlessly he countermanded the Bishop's orders to the Teachers.

An explanatory letter from Father Polidori reached the perplexed Bishop posthaste. At his command, Father stated, the Teachers had not returned to Montefiascone. The Bishop had been deceived by Canon Cocchi whose designs were devious. The Canon wished to rob the Teachers not only of their home but also of their good reputation.

True, the Teachers had been sick, but now, in the summer of 1724, they were in perfect health. However, Father Polidori continued, even during their illness, they had not closed the School, had not neglected their prayer-life, had not ceased to minister to the parish-at-large. The Teachers had taken turns to rest and work so as not to interrupt their apostolate. The good wrought by the Teachers through the Schools was indisputable.

He urged the Bishop to retract his orders. Only he as Bishop had the power, Father reminded him, to justify the Teachers' decision not to return to Montefiascone. The eyes and ears of the town, on both sides of the issue, awaited his episcopal response.

Lucy also went to the Bishop. Her perceptive analysis of the situation bore out Father Polidori's arguments and opened the Bishop's eyes to the truth.

Only a small minority, influenced by the Canon, resented the Bishop's forthcoming decision. Subtly they continued to wage their campaign of hatred. Lucy and her Teachers continued to suffer the sting of their revenge with patience and forgiveness. Their heroic love in the face of so much animosity was a lesson the women never forgot.

In Valentano, Canon Paul Vaiani served as the devil's ally against Lucy. Obsessed with jealousy, the Canon nourished one all-absorbing goal: the destruction of Lucy through her Schools. He planned to accomplish this objective by founding his own Schools, his own congregation. He had winning ways with the women: He knew how to flatter them into following him wherever he led them.

Unsuspecting women gathered around him, convinced of his

good intentions. After a brief, superficial formation period, he invested them as members of the third order of St. Catherine of Siena. The simple women, unaware of his real motives, sought extended community experiences with Lucy's Teachers in prayer and in the study of Christian doctrine.

Canon Vaiani was determined to destroy any and whatever residue of respect his congregation held for the Teachers. He began by inundating their minds with calumny and slander against Lucy and her Teachers. Lacking depth, they believed him and joined him by spreading the evil news to all who would listen. The ground work accomplished, Vaiani took the final and most destructive step: he opened his own schools. An unthinking mob, completely won over by the Canon's rhetoric, followed and obeyed his every directive.

Lucy confronted a hardened people; her words bounced back to her unaccepted. Lucy's Schools in Valentano emptied out to Vaiani's. Still the Teachers maintained their dignity; never did they stoop to detract or disparage Vaiani's schools.

The new congregation, however, could not cope with its fast-found success. Drunk with power, they forgot their reason for being. Their life of prayer became a sham; their total deterioration followed rapidly. Horrendous scandals ravaged the countryside! Finally those people who had not been taken in could bear no more. In desperation they called upon the Bishop to visit their town and put an end to the disaster.

The aging Bishop shared the pain experienced by Lucy and her Teachers. He minced no words in his action against Canon Vaiani whom he punished severely. He disbanded the new congregation. Externally, it was all over for Vaiani and his congregation. But they had planted seeds of discord, of suspicion. It would be a long time before such seeds could be completely uprooted.

Lucy's Schools struggled to recapture the original fervor, but it could only happen slowly, very slowly. Valentano left a deep wound in Lucy's heart.

In Arlena, on the other hand, the people loved and respected their Teachers. Yet even in that town the Teachers suffered at the hands of a monomaniac. On August 7, 1724, a group of girls accompanied their Teachers—Agostina Tortori and Anna Maria Tenti—to the LaPiana fountain to fetch water. One girl balanced a bucket on her head; another carried a towel, another an apron. Happily they walked the country road, laughing and singing. It was a wonderful day.

Suddenly, out of nowhere it seemed, a huge red-haired man, Agostino Di Simone, better known as Rossoni, blocked their path. His eyes blazed with hatred. Armed with clubs, he dared them to advance. They had no right, he claimed, to take water; it was his property. (Of course it was an unjust claim.)

Lunging forward, he pulled the apron off one of the girls and grabbed the other's towel. Calmly Agostina remarked, "Thanks be to God that only we are prevented from taking this water."

Her serene comment maddened him more. Waving his club, he promised revenge, and then disappeared.

Frightened, the teachers and students quickly filled the bucket and turned toward home . . . when there he was again! This time he carried a gun. "I'll fix you now," he screamed. He fired . . . and missed! The children screamed. Then they began to pray aloud to the Virgin Mary.

Anna Maria, with extraordinary courage and presence of mind, grabbed the gun and pointed the barrel away from the children. Rossoni fired again—into nothing; it was his last bullet. Screaming madly, he left them, vowing he would succeed next time.

News of the episode spread quickly. The town of Arlena rose up in arms, determined to vindicate their Teachers. Only the hand of God prevented them from lynching Di Simone. The authorities finally captured him and imprisoned him in Montefiascone.

Lucy rushed to Arlena. Her Teachers were certainly shaken; their greatest concern, however, had been the children. The children crowded around Lucy, anxious to share their frightful experience. They were convinced, they exclaimed, that the Virgin Mary had saved them, for it was to her they had turned in that awful hour. Lucy's presence among the Teachers and students healed the last bit of fright lingering within them. She made them promise to pray for Di Simone's conversion. Their spontaneous "yes" made every agony worthwhile.

In Piansano, Lucy and her Teachers suffered persecution from 1726 to 1730. Anna and Laura Lottieri, noted for their sanctity but not for their intelligence, directed the School there. They came from peasant stock with limited culture, but they had boundless love and zeal; the people looked upon them as saints. Father Domenic Parri, one of the curates, did not share the common feeling.

He was a brilliant, well-educated man from a wealthy family. Pride devoured him. He looked upon the Lottieri Teachers as scum, too far beneath his superior intellectual powers. He resented the Teachers' popularity among the people. Lucy's obvious influence in Piansano infuriated him. Father Domenic was an ambitious man; the priesthood to him was only a means to power and prestige. Obstacles to that end he removed without any scruples.

Keenly aware of the two Teachers' limited intelligence, he set a trap to catch them in doctrinal error. For this purpose he assigned a Capuchin priest to attend the daily mental prayer sessions the Lottieri Teachers conducted. He warned him to find fault, even if he had to twist the truth. The Capuchin, no less unscrupulous, managed to create a believable fable founded on nothing. The Teachers, he declared loudly, were teaching falsehoods. Both men skirted questions which sought to pinpoint specifics, but rumors spread.

On Holy Thursday, Anna approached the confessional to receive the sacrament of Penance. In a dramatic show of anger, the Capuchin stepped out of the confessional and ordered her out. He insulted her publicly, threw invectives at her, called her ignorant, and declared her a heretic. In a voice rasped with hostility, he threatened to denounce her to the Holy Office.

Anna bowed her head in confusion; she could not understand hatred. Witnesses to the scene suffered with the Teachers; the evil rumors had failed to take deep root in Piansano.

Lucy and the pastor recognized the source of the problem. The Teachers' great success with the Holy Rosary Society and the Child

Jesus Devotion had interfered with Father Parri's ambition to make his particular group the only power in the parish. In fact his society had become extinct as a result of the other societies' phenomenal growth.

Father Parri's ego was deflated by the very women he despised. To whitewash his failure he began to circulate ugly rumors insinuating immoral relations between the pastor and the Teachers. To support his implications, he suborned an ignorant country priest, Father Bartholomew Brizzi, and seven lay people. He mesmerized them into signing a statement claiming they had witnessed scandalous behavior between the pastor and the Teachers.

Up to this point the people of Piansano had considered Father Parri's jealousy and pride distasteful, to be sure, but they had not expected him to stoop so low. Their retaliation was immediate and strong. They formulated a petition in defense of their Teachers. All but the seven lay people, the Capuchin, and the antagonist himself signed the statement. They forwarded the petition to the Bishop and asked him to proclaim judgment on the evil priest.

The Teachers had never informed the Bishop about their problem with Father Parri; they did not want to discredit him before his superior. Furthermore they had thought the problem would disappear. Jealousy was beyond their comprehension.

The Bishop did not condone the Teachers' reticence. In a letter announcing his coming visit, he voiced his displeasure. He reminded them of his abiding concern for them and the necessity to be kept informed.

Bishop Bonaventura traveled to Piansano to call the calumniators to order and to defend the Teachers' names. It was not difficult to dispel the calumny Father Parri had circulated about the Teachers. With the exception of the few dissenters, the people of Piansano were positive of the Teachers' innocence.

Father Parri, however, never relented. He and his small following planted thorns in every project the Teachers initiated or were involved in. The two Teachers lived from one torture to the next, never sure what each new day would bring.

Lucy's constant support and encouragement strengthened Anna and Laura during those four years of agony. But their patience bore much fruit. It was in this town, from this School of suffering, that another saint was reared. Her name was Lucia Berlini (whose cause for beatification is now in process), an exemplary student, Lucia spent her formative years in Anna and Laura's School.

Suffering and persecution paved every step of the way for Lucy and her patient community. For the love of the Crucified Christ, they joyfully accepted even derision.

On May 7, 1728, on the very day Bishop Bonaventura visited the School in Marta, a woman named Domenica Angela ridiculed the Teachers publicly in the presence of the Bishop. Another woman placed herself in front of the Collegiate Church and covered the Teacher with spittle and insults. Rosa Latini was the Teacher, the same one who had left the Institute to join the Teaching Branch of the Divine Love Congregation.

(While Rose had been a member of the Divine Love Congregation, her brother-in-law had become very ill. Her sister had written begging her to return home to help during the vacation period. When Rose had asked Don Morani's permission, he had replied that whoever left the monastery could never return, no matter what reason instigated the departure. Rose had not believed he meant it, especially since he lacked personnel for the School. So she had left to go to her sister's home during her vacation.

Rose had discovered, much to her consternation, that Morani intended every word he had said. Disillusioned by Don Morani's rigor and inhumanity, Rose had asked readmission into Lucy's Institute. Lucy had welcomed her back. Upon her return Rose had experienced only mercy and compassion from Lucy and the Teachers.)

No wonder then that Rose Latini could turn mercifully toward her persecutors, bless them, and pray the words, "May God make you saints." But her meekness did not move the offenders; hardened men joined the women in their mockery. Rose and her companion continued to bless them.

Lucy bore every pain inflicted upon her Teachers. Humbly she prayed:

I willingly accept this little suffering from God's hands. I would accept even the Cross and be crucified for Jesus Christ, as He willingly did for me, because it is not proper for a bride to be happy while her Spouse is in pain and suffering.

Her willingness to suffer, however, did not deter her from using every means which prudence suggested to relieve her Teachers' suffering and to safeguard the Schools. Yet she was solicitous for one thing only, that God's will be fulfilled. In one of her letters to the Princess Altieri, she wrote, "We are always disposed to adore the divine dispositions because they are always directed to our good. May the Lord's will be done. I am resigned."

The Schools, however, were not the only targets in the general persecutions. Unscrupulous churchmen, determined to destroy Lucy herself, attacked her good name and integrity.

At the time of the Cardinal's death, Canon Luca Corneli and Canon Alexander Mazzinelli were the first two dignitaries in the diocese. Into their hands the Cardinal had entrusted the administration of the school funds. Unwilling to assume the burden of maintaining eleven Schools on the meager inheritance, they had relegated the responsibility to Lucy. They recognized and admired her practical nature, her ingenuity, and, above all, her faith in Divine Providence. Only Lucy, they agreed, could manage successfully on the mere pittance she had inherited from the Cardinal.

Lucy proved worthy of their faith in her. With the foresight and keen mind of a good businesswoman, she had invested wisely, had purchased real estate to give stability to the Schools had, in short, more than tripled what she had been willed. As one body, the Teachers had scrimped and saved to make ends meet during those first years after Barbarigo's death.

Foreseeing the possibility of future administrators' being disinterested in the welfare of the Schools, Lucy had taken precautionary measures. She kept the record of funds received from Barbarigo and his nephew, Francis, strictly separated from those accured from her own dowry, her sister's bequest, and the monies earned by the Schools.

Actually no dichotomy existed in Lucy's mind between her Schools and her own personal funds. To Lucy nothing was hers personally. But in her wisdom she judged it proper and prudent to secure the future of the Schools against usurpers. The account in her name was the Schools' insurance policy. Should her premonitions be correct, these funds would safeguard the stability of her Schools. Her prudence inspired this separation of funds; her intuition confirmed it.

Bishop Bonaventura, in the very first year of his episcopacy, had appointed Monsignor Sebastiano Antonini his Vicar General. From the very beginning Lucy had read the jealousy, envy and avarice registered in the Vicar's heart. During the twenty-six years Antonini served the Bishop, he exerted tremendous influence on Bonaventura. Now, in the latter's old age, Antonini held the reins of power.

Antonini hated Lucy, resented the trust and esteem bestowed on her by the Pope and bishops. That Bishop Bonaventura supported and maintained the Schools at his own expense exasperated Antonini. Avarice gnawed at him and fed his hatred.

As Vicar, Antonini also functioned as judge for civil and criminal cases. Among those brought to court were pietistic hypocrites who *flaunted* their religiosity in order to cheat the simple. Antonini's experiences with these imposters made him suspicious of all pious people. He made no effort to separate the wheat from the chaff, so Lucy suffered this judgment also.

Antonini's legal eyes shrewdly observed Lucy; to him she was an astute businesswoman, deceptively guised in the holy habit. On the other hand, he envied her success and coveted the funds she had gained for the Schools.

But as long as Canon Corneli and Canon Mazzinelli lived, Antonini's hands were tied. So Antonini waited and vented his rancor on anyone who favored or protected Lucy. Woe to those unfortunate victims! If they fell into an illegality, he had no mercy on them.

For thirteen years Antonini bided his time. Then, on April 20, 1720, Canon Corneli died. It was the opening Antonini had waited for; the time had come for him to take action.

For Lucy it was a sad moment; she had lost a dear friend and loyal supporter. Corneli had been like a father to her; he had reminded her so much of Cardinal Barbarigo. How often Lucy had turned to him for counsel in business affairs; he had understood her plight. His influence had helped her in crucial moments. Now he was gone; now new dangers awaited her Schools. Another "now" was calling forth another "yes," and Lucy pronounced it . . . trustingly.

Antonini captured the moment and conquered. He induced Bishop Bonaventura to nominate Canon Antonio Falisci to replace Corneli. Falisci was Antonini's right-hand man and wholly subservient to him; Antonini had but to command.

Antonini's first order directed Falisci to Lucy to claim his rights as administrator of school funds. He stated that though Corneli had not wanted to be bothered with the duty imposed on him by the will, he, Falisci, considered it a responsibility he could not avoid. In fact, he continued, he intended to administer all the school funds.

Lucy did not yield! His demand was unjust and unethical. Calmly she presented her reasons for refusing. Cardinal Barbarigo, she pointed out, had stated that only those goods left to the School by him and his nephew were to be administered by chancery officials. According to the will, she continued, the two diocesan executives were to preside in association with the finance committee the Cardinal had set up in the Seminary. But, she noted, the Bishop had suppressed the finance committee. Therefore, the previous stipulation was also no longer in effect. If, however, the Bishop judged the statement concerning the two dignitaries' right to administer still relevant, then she would hand over *only* that which Barbarigo and his nephew had willed to the Schools. She could not, she insisted, relinquish that which she had gained with her own dowry, her sister's bequest, or through the sacrifices her Teachers had made in the Schools. Then she threw him a penetrating question! Why were they assuming their responsibility now, thirteen years later? Why had they not burdened themselves with the Schools' maintenance when the funds were nil?

Lucy's logic and clairvoyance incensed Falisci. Leaving her abruptly, he headed for Antonini's residence. What should he do now?

A suave Antonini knocked at the door of St. Margaret and asked to speak to Lucy. He informed her that the Bishop had ordered that she act according to the will; she should give to Falisci the right to administer only the goods left by the Cardinal and his nephew.

Her superior, the Bishop, had spoken; for Lucy there was now no alternative. She was grateful, moreover, that he had not extended the order to include the second account. But the end of the matter was not in view, nor would it be in Lucy's lifetime and all because of a human mistake Lucy had made a decade ago.

On March 6, 1709, Lucy had bought an olive grove in the territory of Celleno, using the last fifty *scudi* of the six-hundred *scudi* left to her by Barbarigo. Inadvertently she had registered the purchase in the account under her name. It was a mistake of inscription, nothing else. Lucy, who lived only for her Schools, who had already donated nine-hundred *scudi* of her own to them, certainly had no intention of appropriating anything for herself. Yet this act, interpreted in legal terms, was a fraud, a usurpation of goods.

On scrutinizing the accounts Lucy had submitted, Falisci found no mention of the last fifty *scudi*. Where had it gone? Antonini and Falisci capitalized on the "unmistakable evidence," refusing to call it an "error of inscription." With the rapidity of a strawfire, the infamous calumny spread far and wide—"embezzler, fraud, hypocrite." So well-worded, so well-argued was the slander that even her old friend, Mazzinelli, succumbed to it. His subsequent alliance with Antonini and Falisci persuaded even the good people. One by one, they turned their backs on Lucy.

Bishop Bonaventura was torn between his esteem for Lucy and his dependence on Antonini. In an effort to vindicate Lucy's honor, he asked Lucy to submit both accounts to Falisci to demonstrate how well she had managed with so little. His intention was good; the end result was a tragedy. Greed blinded the two men to the true story behind the figures. They ignored the first pages, written in red. Only the final sheets interested them. Here were recorded the assets Lucy had gained for her Institute. Avarice governed the hearts of these unprincipled men. Mentally they already possessed the hard-earned properties and funds Lucy and her Teachers had struggled to obtain.

On June 11, 1727 Lucy was summoned to the diocesan tribunal. Her judge—Monsignor Sebastian Antonini; her accuser—Canon Falisci; her "crime"—embezzlement of funds.

Lucy faced her accusers! She heard their voices coming from afar: "Condemned . . . hand over all goods . . . all funds . . . sign declaration that you will never question . . . interfere . . . suggest . . . or appeal to a higher authority . . . regarding administration of both accounts. It is the order of your Bishop, your Superior."

Stupefied by the cruelty avarice generates, Lucy signed the declaration in obedience to her lawful Superior. Defamed, hated, without honor, Lucy left the courtroom. Her dignified silence spoke volumes, but no one heard her.

And Lucy prayed: "It is true, that by the grace of God I have not committed the horrors I am accused of and which are publicly declared. But, nevertheless, I have been and am presently so unworthy of God that I really deserve a thousand times worse. Give me patience, Father. Do with me as You will. May You be praised a thousand times over! Blessed be Your Holy Name."

Notwithstanding her total abandonment to God. Lucy's delicate and sensitive nature was deeply wounded. The cells of her body festered and deteriorated. A slow, continuous fever, accompanied by intense pain, assailed her. At the tender insistence of her Teachers, Lucy consulted a doctor. The diagnosis revealed a pernicious cancer. Only Viterbo offered treatments to cancer patients in the Montefiascone area. But Lucy was penniless and Falisci coldly insensitive. Only Mazzinelli sympathized; he had, to his embarrassment, finally awakened to the treachery perpetrated by Antonini. He could not do enough for Lucy to compensate for his short-lived mistrust. It was he, therefore, who obtained the money Lucy needed to go to Viterbo.

Every time the full extent of the document she had signed cut through her pain—every time she envisaged the future deprivation of her Schools, an agony more violent than the previous one engulfed her. A deep sense of justice moved her to readjust the state of affairs. But Lucy's plea for mercy fell upon stony hearts; the Vicar simply flung before her the signed document.

A more devastating attack of the sickness seized Lucy; fever consumed her; intense pains robbed her of sleep. But things could not destroy her. Someone overpowered the evil, strengthened her spirit, sustained her, invigorated her. Turning to Him whom she loved beyond measure, Lucy spoke these words: "Even if all the men of the world with all the demons of hell, persecuted me and desired my ruin, I firmly hope that God will never abandon me. He alone will give me the strength to overcome them all, because He is merciful."

In the embrace of His strength-filled love, Lucy carried on her apostolate. She persisted in her teaching, preaching, visiting the Schools, governing her community. Her face, alight with zeal, belied her agony. When her frail body refused to stir, her bedroom became a classroom, pulpit, listening room. Her words cast out fear; her touch healed; her presence blessed.

Her illness, however, did not mellow her persecutors. Their subterfuges never ceased; mercilessly one attack followed rapidly upon the other. Yet Lucy did not despair, nor was she frightened. Her heart filled with hope, she exclaimed: "Even though all men would leave me and I were abandoned and forsaken by all my friends and relatives, I have strong hope that my God will never leave me because He will still be my Father."

To her Teachers, who shared her every pain, she said: "I want nothing else but His Divine Glory. Even if they ruin Lucy, what of it? They will have done nothing but crush a little woman. I fear nothing."

Having handed in all documents pertaining to the administration of the school funds, Lucy was left without documentary evidence to defend her own conduct against future charges. The actions of her enemies, on the other hand, could not be checked.

Exploitation began immediately. Lucy was forced to hand over all cash on hand and all of the wheat and barley held in reserve. When bills came due at the end of the month, Falisci denied her request for the stipulated amount.

Lucy read their objective; they intended to drive the Schools against the wall, forcing them to close. The Schools, at the mercy of this scheme, would die a "natural" death. But there were blind spots in her adversaries' plans, spots they had not foreseen.

They were battling against women dedicated to a crucified Christ, against women taught by a woman in love with that suffering Christ. They fought a losing battle.

Lucy never ceased in her search to relieve the sufferings of her Teachers and the Schools. Sensitive to the sacramental character of the priesthood, however, she desisted from initiating public action against them. But she did not hesitate to seek private counsel and assistance from prudent and influential persons.

In a letter to her dear friend, Princess Altieri, she wrote:

> I have had a thought, but it seems foolish. If a zealous person could be found to write to the chief dignitaries of Rome and say to them, "There is a rumor that the diocesan Schools of Montefiascone are in ruin. Please investigate and give both parties involved the right to give reasons." We could then work freely.

At the instigation of the Princess, the Pope's Almoner did go to Montefiascone towards the end of October, 1730. Realizing that Lucy was innocent, he suggested that Lucy prepare a memorandum on the whole matter. Lucy thought it more prudent to commission a legal expert to write it. In fact, she preferred not seeing it. It was another tragic error. The lawyer omitted necessary items and facts; the omissions occasioned new recriminations against Lucy.

When the Holy See sent the memorandum to the Bishop for explanation, Bonaventura was hurt and angry: hurt, because the document made no mention of the money he had personally contributed every year; angry, because the document asked for the abrogation of one of his official acts. (On December 27, 1727, the Bishop, at the instigation of Antonini, had added a third member to the School Fund Administration Committee, Canon Angelo Processi.) Burning with indignation, the Bishop left for Tarquinia. He passed the memorandum on to his Vicar, asking him to explain the situation to Rome using facts and figures.

A written diatribe followed. The discrepancy between the two reports paralyzed the Almoner's hands. In Montefiascone, the work of exploitation continued with impunity.

Pressed by authorities in Rome to write another statement, Lucy wrote to the Princess: "I beg you to hinder the writing of any statement. Help me by preventing this. If another action is taken, my adversaries will enforce the closing of the Schools. His will be done. He will provide."

Lucy, steadfast in her faith in Divine Providence, remained calm and serene. In a letter written to Princess Altieri on January 30, 1731, she remarked: "The whole matter still remains in the dark. The blackness of my sins must be the reason; but since this is the Lord's own business, He will take care of it. We, on our part, will do all we can, because the mercy of God will not fail those who trust in Him."

The Roman Teachers, heavy hearted with grief over Lucy's afflictions, took action. They solicited the assistance of the Pope's Almoner, Monsignor Nicolo Albini, their ecclesiastical superior who held great respect for Lucy. He summoned Lucy to Rome, where, he promised, excellent doctors would be engaged to examine her at his own expense. Lucy accepted the invitation, primarily to obtain relief for her Schools in the Montefiascone diocese.

While in Rome Lucy wrote to Princess Altieri, asking her for a half-hour of her time to discuss the grave situation of her Schools. The Princess, concerned about Lucy's health, volunteered to go to her to spare her the agony of traveling. At least once a week, the Princess returned; often Princess Pallavicini accompanied her. Their visits consoled Lucy, not only because they were beloved friends, but also because they had committed themselves to rescue the Schools in Montefiascone. They were very much affected by the injustices inflicted upon Lucy and her Schools; Lucy's cause had become theirs.

The Roman Teachers shared their abundance with their suffering, deprived sister-Teachers in Montefiascone. Their uninterrupted communication with them lifted the spirits of those long-suffering women. Their benefactions and solicitude rounded out the edges of their poverty, making it seem less burdensome.

The nobility of Rome, in a movement inaugurated by the Princess Altieri, supplied the deprived Schools with the bare necessities—at least. Their concerned effort to promote and restore justice awakened the interest of influential persons in the Vatican. Lucy, however, did not live to witness the effects of this widespread movement.

In July, 1730, Lucy, preoccupied with the welfare of her Teachers in Montefiascone, left Rome to return home. Her illness was beyond human control; the treatment received had only aggravated the pain. Her Roman Teachers wept inconsolably at her departure! They could not imagine a future without her.

From Montefiascone, Lucy pleaded her case again to the Princess: "Humbly I salute the Prince to whom I recommend the suffering Schools. Whether I live or die, I entrust this great apostolate to him. Tell him to take care of my exhausted Teachers; they have suffered so much."

On November 29, 1731, Lucy wrote her last letter to the Princess. Its contents reveal her complete detachment from all earthly interests, her ardent desire to go home—to her eternal home with her Divine Spouse.

> I beg you to let me know how you are, because I am a little worried, remembering you were not quite well when I left Rome. I am not so well myself. Please, Excellency, ask God to forgive me, and having forgiven me, to take me whenever He pleases. He is all our Good; outside of Him there is no other Good. If we as Christians had the true light of God, we—like our Lady—would look at death with longing. But we are so blind; we love this miserable life more than the true life which is full of bliss. Good-bye, dear Princess. My most humble regards to the Prince. Tell him I recommend my poor Schools to his care.

The next day, November 30, 1731, Lucy suffered a fainting spell while at School. When she recovered consciousness, she refused to go to bed. The ladies had already gathered for meditation; she could not send them away without speaking to them. It was the last meditation she gave, on her feet. The women remembered every word of that ardent message to their dying day.

Drained from the exertion, Lucy finally yielded to the demands of her tormented body. Her cancerous tumor burst open; excessive hyperaesthesia plus contraction of all nerves brought complete paralysis.

Her gifted tongue and brilliant mind, however, remained unaffected.

13

Pronouncing the Final Yes

> *My God, I love You so much,*
> *that I desire my bones to be*
> *lamps, my blood oil and my*
> *flesh a wick and that I, as a*
> *lighted lamp burn and consume*
> *myself entirely in Your love.*
> —Lucy Filippini

LUCY LINGERED on four more months, radically dependent upon others—nakedly poor, in fact and in spirit—clear-visioned. Against the background of excruciating pains, she reviewed her life, a kaleidoscopic blend of work and prayer, of successes and failures, of joys and sorrows—variegated manifestations of God's will and Providence. Pain-racked hours trans-substantiated into Psalms of Praise . . . of thanksgiving . . . of petition . . . of mercy.

From the very beginning, her heavenly Father had called her by name . . . He had sent the Cardinal, his ambassador, to guide her on the way . . . He had entrusted her with a sacred mission . . . He had delegated her to lift womanhood to the height of Mary . . . He had gifted her to speak His word:

—to teach the ignorant . . .

—to preach His love and mercy . . .

—to touch hearts . . .

—to convert sinners . . .

—to incarnate Him!

He had enriched her with associates, heirs to His gifts. He had graced them with His own contemplative nature. He had gifted them with his own dynamism.

Exultantly, her voice prayed the "Te Deum": "We praise Thee, O God: we acknowledge Thee to be the Lord."*

Lucy's jubilant voice sang out her praise to God. Her Teachers, believing she was pronouncing her last "yes," rushed to her bedside. Her eyes bright with tears, she smiled her welcome; she loved them so much. Humbly she reminisced about their sacred heritage aloud.

Joy-filled pain contracted and expanded their hearts as they drank in her power-filled, prophetic words. All the grace-filled yesterdays . . . all the promised Christ-ever-present tomorrows . . . all converged into one and became eternal todays for the loving community gathered around Lucy Filippini.

Then, in the strength of her jubilation, they also raised their voices in song:

> We beseech Thee, therefore, help
> Thy servants whom Thou hast
> redeemed with Thy Precious Blood.
>
> Make them to be numbered with Thy
> Saints, in glory everlasting.
>
> Save Thy people, O Lord, and
> bless Thine inheritance.
>
> And rule them, and exalt them forever.*

Lucy's face, bathed in the light of Christ's Spirit, announced her ecstatic union with her Beloved. Clear-eyed she reviewed each decision she had made.

In the selflessness of her "now," she admitted the painful shedding of her self-centered "then." She recalled the sound of her quivered "yes," She relived each agonized admission of weakness, she recalled the glorious avowal of her stark emptiness before the all-powerful God.

Memories rushed upon her—nostalgic thoughts—memorable annunciations of God's will, of His providential love, grateful memories of her *Forever Yes.*

*"Te Deum," *The Catholic Encyclopedia for School and Home,* vol 10. (New York: McGraw-Hill Book Company, 1965), p. 563.

—Her first schools . . . Her treasured association with the Cardinal . . . Their exultant joy every time Christ became Lord of His people—every time a family accepted Christ into their family circle—every time they opened another School!

—Her beloved Teachers—Vincenza, Anna, Laura, Rosa, Maria, all of them . . . their spirit of sacrifice, their faith-filled lives, their maturity, their profound understanding of mission . . . their enthusiasm, their unity of vision, their zeal . . . their poverty . . . their humiliations and sufferings!

—The laughing faces of her students everywhere . . . the young and the old . . . the alumnae . . . their response to God's challenges . . . their dynamic role in a changing society . . . their determined commitment to be Christ-bearers.

Visitors constantly interrupted her musings. Her Teachers, scattered in fifty-two Schools, visited her during the afternoon hours and on weekends. They wanted to memorize every feature of her beloved face, register indelibly every message she spoke from her bed of pain, so they could then pass her on to future generations. Pious women continued to come for morning and evening meditation; her sweet endurance gave them strength. Young girls sought her counsel; their eyes begged her to live; they needed her as their mothers had. Her numerous priest friends came to console her but left consoled themselves.

Bishop Bonaventura, extremely saddened at the possibility of her death, visited her often. He ordered that her name be mentioned at every Mass offered in the diocese. He asked the people to pray for a miracle. The good man was beginning to discover facts he still hesitated to believe. (Shortly after Lucy's death, Bonaventura dismissed Angelo Processi. On September 17, 1733, six months after Lucy's death, Falisci died. One year later, the Bishop dismissed the Vicar General and sent him back home to his own town where he died in obscurity.)

Lucy's sister, Elizabeth, and brother John Francis, were frequent visitors. In recent years John Francis, like his sister, Elizabeth, had become one of the Schools' greatest benefactors.

On December 9, 1731, John Francis dropped in to see Lucy, laden with gifts he knew she could use for her Schools. He was God-sent, for that very day Lucy had learned that her Teachers in Gradoli needed financial aid to purchase a site and the required material to build a wine cellar. Her brother's gift of twenty *scudi* was speedily forwarded to Father Polidori who had informed Lucy of the need. For her Teachers in Gradoli, the wine cellar became a shrine to her sensitive consideration of them.

In between visits, Lucy continued to count her blessings. Gratefully, she praised God for her failures, her humiliations, her adversities, her moments of crisis, of anxiety and fear, of frustration and opposition.

Only when she had contemplated each burden, each humiliation, each adversity as the loving will of God—only at that moment in time had her yoke been sweet, her burden light.

Her failure in the monastery had stripped her of all vanity, had taught her to trust God alone, had strengthened the bond of friendship among her Teachers, had freed her to be herself.

Accusations hurled against her had cut down her pride, had made her indifferent to human respect. They had judged her Quietist . . . embezzler . . . fraud! They had judged Him blasphemer . . . fool . . . fraud! If He, why not she?

Her "error of inscription" had emptied her totally. Her whole being had become a yawning emptiness only God could fill. Her failure had rescued her people, had delivered them of their complacency. Her failure had forced them to become value-oriented, God-centered people.

Her failure to prove her innocence had flung her irrevocably into the arms of Divine Providence. Her Teachers and future Teachers would make that lesson their heritage.

She had used every means prudence suggested to restore her Schools financially, but she had failed! God would not fail! Into His hands she placed His works, trustingly.

Lucy, the invalid, lived each moment fully. She prayed night and day: prayer of service, prayer of gratitude, prayer of humble acceptance, prayer of contemplation. No complaint passed her lips! She placed no imposition on the Teachers. She accepted their loving ministrations gratefully, never asking for anything, never refusing anything.

131

Asked how she could bear so much pain joyfully, she answered, "Only by the grace of God." A simple woman . . . a simple answer.

One of Lucy's Teachers wrote to Father Di Simone, "Lucy continues to suffer tremendously. When the doctor informed her that death was imminent, her joy exploded. Now, however, she is saddened; time seems too long. In fact it seems like a thousand years to her. She finds her joy in the thought of heaven, even in the midst of excruciating pain."

Yet Lucy never stopped living, never ceased caring for God's people. When Lucy learned that financial disaster had struck one of the women she knew, she took immediate action. A donation, recently acquired, was quickly placed into an envelope and delivered to her by one of the Teachers. Along with it she also sent a box of candy she had just that day received from the Princess.

On another day her Teachers informed her that a woman, frustrated to the point of despair, threatened to commit suicide. Only her paralytic condition prevented Lucy from rushing to her. Placing the woman in God's hands, she called for her dear friend, Abbot Mazzinelli, begging him to hasten to the poor woman. Many hours dragged by before the good Abbot succeeded in calming her. Discovering that poverty contributed to the woman's disturbance, Mazzinelli provided for her material needs as well. A tranquil woman attended Lucy's evening meditation session the following day in thanksgiving.

Lucy wavered between life and death during the first two weeks of March, 1732. On the feast of St. Joseph, March 19th, Lucy awakened before dawn. The beautiful words spoken by Zachariah welled up within and poured out of her ecstatically:

Blessed be the Lord the God of Israel
because he was visited and ransomed his people.
All this is the work of the kindness of our God;
he, the Dayspring, shall visit us in his mercy
To shine on those who sit in darkness and in the shadow
of death, to guide our feet into the way of peace.

(Luke 1:68, 78, 79)

132

Turning to the young Teacher kneeling at her bedside, she announced: "I am going home on the 25th of March. My God, My All! Here I am, Your handmaid. Your will be done, forever!"

Later that same day a more devastating paralysis attacked her, stilling her voice forever.

For six days Lucy remained in a coma, her eyes closed to all but the God who lived within her.

All day, all night her Teachers kept vigil. Several were around her bed; several in the Cathedral; others in the School chapel. For six days the people of Montefiascone prayed incessantly, beseeching God to spare her. The streets and alleys of Montefiascone were dumb with pain. Children gathered in groups to pray or to relate stories about their saintly Teacher.

Grandmothers remembered her youthful days as student, as young Teacher. Families knelt and prayed the Rosary. They fasted; they made sacrifices. They wept!

Teachers, strained with contained sorrow, reported her condition periodically.

A few minutes before the clock struck noon, Lucy awakened from her deep coma. It was March 25, 1732, feast of the Annunciation of Mary. A brilliant aura suffused Lucy, filling out her wasted cheeks. Opening her eyes wide, she smiled a smile of blissful joy; a yearning sigh escaped her heart! The Cathedral organ across the street pealed out Lucy's favorite hymn, *Ave Maris Stella;* its melody drifted into the room and filled it. His Presence, was all around her; it was within her. Nothing, no one could prevent her from embracing Him! It was her climactic moment!

It was the moment when all the "yesses" of Lucy Filippini's life came together and became her eternal Magnificat, her *Forever Yes.*

EPILOGUE

Long before the Holy Roman Catholic Church officially declared Lucy Filippini a saint, her countrymen had already proclaimed her Holy Teacher—Venerable Lucy. Those whose lives she had touched directly knew the power of her intercession; they needed no further confirmation. Those who learned of her through others were no less convinced of her sanctity, of her powerful mediation.

From her heavenly home, Lucy never stopped caring for the sick, the suffering, the despairing. During the viewing of her mortal remains immediately after her death, Lucy carried on her apostolate of mercy without interruption. A young woman, Margaret di Domenico de Santi, approached the casket where Lucy lay in the Cathedral of Montefiascone, picked up Lucy's right hand which was still flexible and soft, and touched it to her throat. Margaret was suffering from tuberculosis of the lymphatic glands. Her parents had taken her to the best doctors. Every remedy then known to medical science had been tried. All had been in vain. But Margaret was confident that Lucy could obtain her cure. She had faith in Lucy's tremendous power with God. Margaret's faith was rewarded; she left the Cathedral totally cured of her tubercular condition.

Another woman suffering from a severe throat infection was also healed. Still another woman edged close to the coffin, cut off a tiny piece of Lucy's dress and applied the cloth to her paralyzed arm. Immediately she was able to move her arm. From that moment she was completely cured.

Miracles, too many to mention, continued to be performed through Lucy's intercession from generation to generation. Lucy Filippini's spirit continued to live among her Teachers and people. For them, going to Lucy with every need and expecting her to help them obtain whatever favor they asked of her had become a way of life. Lucy was their powerful mediator in heaven; she was their saintly mother, foundress, teacher, friend. Perhaps that was why the Religious Teachers Filippini made no effort to promote her cause for canonization. But there may have been other reasons also: the lack of funds, the frequent and devastating wars in eighteenth and nineteenth century Italy, the political turmoils. Or it may simply have been Divine Providence!

In essence canonization gives no added honor to a person. It merely confirms the glory already being enjoyed by the saint. God confirms the sanctity of a saint to the world only when the life of that person can serve as a model for the particular needs of a given day. The twentieth century had need of a Lucy Filippini. Teachers had lost their sense of mission, schools had become business institutions, and Christian family life was once again on the decline.

One hundred twenty-six years passed after Lucy's burial before there was any thought of opening her grave. Sister Margaret Balducci, Superior General of the Religious Teachers Filippini Institute in Montefiascone, made the formal request and received the necessary permission from the Church authorities.

In the presence of the local ordinary, Bishop Jona, his Pro-Vicar General, his chancellor, three lay witnesses, and a large number of Religious Teachers from Montefiascone and Rome, the grave was officially opened on April 24, 1858.

They found the casket well-preserved. Suppressed excitement pervaded the room as the bishop moved to lift the lid of the casket. What would they find?

Suddenly a thunder of voices shattered the suspense-filled stillness. "Lucy is here. God has preserved her for us."

There she was, the humble maiden of Tarquinia, peacefully sleeping the sleep of the just, her face soft and white, her lips parted ever so slightly in a gentle smile. On her brow lay the bridal wreath, the symbol of her virginity. Though it was an artificial crown of

135

lilies, it filled the air with a lily-like perfume. But more marvelous still were the hyacinths at her feet, as fresh and sweet as they were one hundred and twenty-six years ago.

And what about Lucy's sacred body? Had God preserved it, protected it from the elements? Miracle of miracles! In a voice suffused with awe, Bishop Jona announced the incredible truth: *Lucy Filippini's body was incorrupt,* even though the clothes she wore were practically decomposed.

It was impossible to restrain the Teachers any longer. They wanted to look upon her whom they loved. They wanted to touch her. They were ecstatic. Emotion-filled hours passed by unnoticed; for Lucy's Teachers, time and eternity had fused into one.

Later that day, Lucy's body, clad in new clothes, was again enclosed, this time in a double casket, and buried in the Cathedral. Lucy lay quietly at rest once more; no further move to begin the beatification process was mentioned.

Lucy Filippini herself seems to have taken the first step towards her canonization. One day towards the end of August of 1903, a young student-Teacher, Sr. Mary Donati, lay in bed mortally sick with typhoid fever.

When the nurse went to supper that August evening in 1903, Lucy Filippini entered the room. She smiled upon Sr. Mary, took her hand, and told her she would get well. She also promised Sr. Mary that she would receive her teaching diploma the following year. When Sr. Mary asked Lucy to give the community her spirit, Lucy replied: "Do all things for the glory of God alone."

Then Lucy made a strange request. "Tell your superior to work for my beatification. The Holy Father will take care of the expense."

Humility is truth. Her canonization would glorify the Lord, for it was He who had done great things for her. If God willed to glorify her soul before men, Lucy, whose will was one with the Lord, also desired it. Lucy's request set the process into motion.

Pope Pius X signed the decree for the introduction of the cause of her beatification and canonization on July 10, 1912. On November 25, 1924, Pope Pius XI solemnly declared the virtue of Lucy Filippini as heroic.

On March 21, 1926, the same Pontiff issued the decree approving three miracles among the many obtained from God at the intercessions of Lucy Filippini.

In preparation for the beatification which was to take place that June of 1926, the coffin was once again reopened on March 25, 1926. In His goodness, God had continued to preserve Lucy's body intact. (In fact, to this day Lucy Filippini's body is almost wholly preserved and can be viewed by the faithful in the crypt of the Cathedral in Montefiascone.)

On June 13, 1926, Religious Teachers Filippini from Italy and the United States went to the Basilica of St. Peter in Vatican City to assist at Lucy's beatification. In the beatification decree, Pope Pius XI acclaimed:

> Lucy Filippini, the Holy Teacher, model and molder of Holy Teachers, admirably responded to the times in which Divine Providence placed her and also to the times in which the same Divine Providence recalls her memory to praise her wondrous works and to present her as an example to others.

> Today we present her again to everyone, exhorting all to imitate her now that the need for sound teaching is more urgent than ever. Now that the school has become everything, the place where good and bad can begin, it is more necessary than ever for it to become the basis of truth and of Christian formation, the anteroom of the temple of the Church.*

After the decree of beatification was read, the veil from the Gloria of Bernini was removed to reveal the triumphant picture of Blessed Lucy Fillippini. At the very same instant there was a sudden flash of lights accompanied by thousands of voices gloriously thundering the "Te Deum." Tears of joy prevented many Teachers from participating in the singing. They were transfixed, ecstatic as they fixed their eyes on Lucy's picture.

While the Pope was pronouncing Lucy *"Blessed Lucy,"* Sister Nicolina Gennari, a Teacher in Rome, was miraculously cured through Lucy's intercession of a long-standing ulcerous tuberculosis of the lungs. On June 6th of that year, Anthony Manieri was suddenly and completely cured of bronchopneumonia, again through the mediation of Lucy.

*From the decree, March 21, 1926.

On May 11, 1930, the Holy See officially approved these two new miracles.

On June 22, 1930, Pius XI solemnly inscribed Lucy Filippini in the Annals of the Saints.

Today, many turn to her and pray:

O glorious St. Lucy, who from your heavenly home continue to love souls and recognize their real wants, bestow your clemency upon us who implore your powerful aid. Since during your mortal life, you have not hesitated to succor the poor, heal the sick, and have opened your most sensitive heart to all miseries to alleviate them, do not, therefore, let us depart from you without having obtained our petition. Continue to show us that you still are a most amiable mother to all who have recourse to you in prayer and confide in your holy protection.

And never has anyone who has prayed to her been left unaided, for Saint Lucy Filippini

. . . is an aura of the might of God and a pure effusion of the glory of the Almighty: Therefore nought that is sullied enters into her.

For she is the refulgence of eternal light, the spotless mirror of the power of God, the image of his goodness.

(Wisdom 7:25–26)

BIBLIOGRAPHY

Abbo, Giovanni A., *L'Istituto Delle Maestre Pie Filippini E La Santa Sede.* Roma: Istituto Grafico Tiberino Di Stefano De Luca, 1962.

Bergamaschi, Pietro, *Vita Della Venerabile Lucia Filippini.* Montefiascone: Bagnorea—Scuola Tipografica, 1916.

Bordo, Bernardino N., *Lucia Burlini.* P.P. Passionisti. Nettuno, Italy: Arti Frafiche Neptunia, 1967.

Brief History of the Religious Teachers Filippini. New Jersey: Villa Walsh, 1935.

Di Belmonte, Cardinal Ianuario Granito Pignatelli, *Sacra Rituum Congregatione (Canonizationis B. Lucia Filippini.* Roma: Tipografia Agostiniana, 1929.

Di Simone, Rev. Francesco, *The Life of the Servant of God Lucy Filippini.* Trans. by Sr. Gilda Dal Corso, M.P.F. Rome: 1732.

Marangoni, Giovanni, *Vita Del Servo Di Dio Card. Marco Antonio Barbarigo.* Roma: Pia Societa S. Paolo, Via Grottaperfette, 1930.

Mazzinelli, Alessandro, *Istruzione per Regolamente della Dottrina Cristiana delle Zitelle.* Roma: Tipografia della Rev. Cam. Apostolica, 1868.

New American Bible. New York: Thos. Nelson, Inc., 1971.

New Catholic Encyclopedia. Volume 7. New York: McGraw-Hill, Book Company, 1967.

Rocca, Suor Mafaldina, *Una Luce Nella Chiesa.* Roma: Tipografia Pontificia Vescovile S. Giuseppe, 1969.

Salotti, Monsignor Carlo, *Compendio Della Santa Lucia Filippini.* Roma: Societa Tipografia A. Macioce E Pisani, 1930.

Salotti, Monsignor Carlo, *La Santa Lucia Filippini Fondatrice E Superiora Dell'Instituto Delle Maestre Pie Filippini.* Roma: Societa Tipografia A. Macioce E Pisani, 1930.

Salvadore, Massimo, *Italy.* New Jersey: Prentice-Hall, 1965.